CRUCIAL QUESTIONS
ABOUT HELL

CRUCIAL QUESTIONS ABOUT HELL

Ajith Fernando

CROSSWAY BOOKS • WHEATON, ILLINOIS
A DIVISION OF GOOD NEWS PUBLISHERS

02	01	00	99	98	97	96	95	94
15	14	13	12	11	10	9	8	7	6	5	4	3	2	1

To my parents
B. E. and Malini Fernando
with gratitude for Christian nurture
and encouragement in ministry

TABLE OF

CONTENTS

FOREWORD

In today's secular West *hell*, like *God* and *Christ*, is just a swear word for letting out strong feelings. In the New Testament, however, hell is a destiny: it is humanity's future life as all who oppose God will experience it. In the Old Testament heaven and hell are largely veiled, but Jesus and the apostles speak of both in language of shattering force, so that what they say of heaven will bring tears of joy, while their words about hell will terrify anyone of normal sensitivity.

Jesus and the apostles, like Old Testament psalmists and prophets, take pleasure in the prospect of righteousness being firmly established everywhere through acts of divine judgment, but they do not gloat over their expectation that for some this will mean everlasting hell. They speak of hell only as evangelists speak of it— namely, to issue compassionate warnings against those paths of indifference and impenitence that lead there, and to gain leverage for begging people to open their hearts to redeeming love. So did George Whitefield and Jonathan Edwards, C. H. Spurgeon and D. L. Moody, and all great evangelists of history. So does Billy Graham; and so does Ajith Fernando in this book.

The New Testament depicts hell as a state of conscious pain, comparable to that of burning, in which condemned persons realize (1) how repulsive and guilty in their Maker's eyes was the way they lived on earth; (2) how right was God's penal exclusion of them from his presence and joy; (3) how completely they have now lost all gladness and pleasure; and (4) how unchangeable is their condition. Yet God's banishment of these persons to hell is just, first because it is less than they deserve, and second because hell—existence apart from God, even though this means apart from good too—is what, at deepest level, they actually embraced in this life, so that God's sentence is a ratifying of their own choice: no less, no more.

During this century some Bible-believers have shifted their ground with regard to the assertion of hell. At one time, evangelical Protestants stoutly maintained the unending agony of those who leave this world without Christ against all suggestions of universal salvation or the post-mortem annihilation of the godless, and they enforced the missionary imperative from the viewpoint of such as Hudson Taylor and Amy Carmichael—namely, that all need to hear of Christ because without him all are lost. Today, however, universalism, the doctrine of a finally empty hell, is rampant, and so are theories of salvation through non-Christian religions and of unbelievers being finally snuffed out. Anyone who, like Ajith Fernando, forthrightly affirms the older doctrine is likely to find himself an embarrassment to his own evangelical friends. Emphasis on the lostness of the lost has come to be almost taboo. The shift is startling.

What has caused the change? Has some new biblical wisdom been born, or is it simply that older biblical wisdom has been forgotten or overlaid? The truth is that here as elsewhere the Bible-believing community of the West is off-balance and staggering, just as a pedestrian who has been cannoned into by two or three heavyweight runners would be off-balance and staggering. For western evangelicals live in a post-Christian, human-centered, self-absorbed, feel-good, secular culture which reduces all religion to a private hobby. They face a bewildering plurality of non-Christian religious faiths, and an equally bewildering variety of theologies within the churches. They know that, because of the world population explosion, more non-Christians are alive today than ever before: will all those billions go to hell? The modern passion to find dignity and worth in all religions presses upon them, and their imaginations have been contaminated with the world's disgust at Jonathan Edwards's attempts to make vivid the thought that without Christ we are sinners in the hands of a wrathful (angry) God. Small wonder, then, if current evangelical declarations and delineations of the lostness of everyone without Christ are sometimes shaky and muted. Swimming against the stream can be hard, and being put on the defensive can cause failure of nerve. Yet the teaching of Scripture stands.

Ajith Fernando is an honest writer who knows his stuff and pulls no punches, and this book, though not comfortable, is realistic and health-giving. I am glad to commend it as a word of needed truth for our time, a rallying statement for evangelicals and an arsenal of argument for evangelists. When the badness of the bad news about hell is unmuffled, as it is here, the goodness of the good news about Christ and eternal life shines brighter. For a book which has this effect one cannot but be grateful, and I am sure I shall not be the only one who feels gratitude for what is written in the pages that follow.

J. I. Packer

INTRODUCTION

This book was written out of the conviction that there is an urgent need for the church to reflect seriously on the doctrine of eternal punishment. There are many reasons for this. Firstly, judgment is rarely mentioned in the conversation, witness, and preaching of most Christians today.

Secondly, many who believe that there will be a future judgment do not know how it should be presented to others and are therefore silent about it. Many sensitive Christians today are embarrassed by the way they heard judgment being proclaimed in the past.

Thirdly, the biblical idea of eternal punishment seems to be incompatible with the ideas of God that many people have and with the pluralistic ideals that dominate much social and religious thinking today.

Fourthly, the rapid spread of universalism in the church today calls for a fresh examination of the universalists' case.

Fifthly, many Christians have questions about hell which need to be addressed anew. This need is particularly significant because theories which were once considered heretical, like reincarnation, purgatorial cleansing, a second chance after death, and annihilationism, are gaining ground in Christian circles.

I studied the topic of this book seriously for the first time during my studies at Fuller Theological Seminary, USA, in the mid-seventies where I wrote a thesis for my Master of Theology degree on the topic of universalism. This was subsequently published in India.[1] I soon came to realize that I needed to build on the foundation of what I had already studied and produce a new book which is more readable and relevant to today's situation.

It is difficult to express adequately my gratitude for all that I learned from Dr. Daniel P. Fuller, who was my supervisor at Fuller. Dr. Arthur F. Glasser, also from Fuller, was a great help to me while I was there. Their help continued when I worked on this book.

Much of this book was written while I was on a sabbatical leave with my family at Gordon-Conwell Theological Seminary in the USA. I am grateful to the administration, staff, faculty, and students who enriched our lives in so many ways during our stay. I am particularly indebted to Dr. David F. Wells who arranged this sabbatical for us. This trip was funded through gifts from numerous friends, family members, and organizations whose names are too many to list here but to whom I express our gratitude.

Many theologians helped me through conversations on the phone or in person and through correspondence, even though I was a complete stranger to some of them. In this regard, in addition to Drs. Fuller, Glasser, and Wells, I must mention Drs. Gary Bekker, Donald A. Carson, Robert Coleman, J. D. Douglas, John Gratien, Carl F. H. Henry, Roger Nicole, Ramesh Richard, Krister Sarsingh, Jerry Walls, Warren Webster, and Matthias Zanheiser.

Despite the help of these scholars, I do not claim to have written a top-level theological work on hell. The need for a theologian to take up that task still remains. What we have here is a biblical study by one actively involved in evangelism, who has studied the Scriptures and has, over a long period, attempted to reflect seriously on the issues related to the topic of hell. I have avoided using technical theological terms in this book, and I hope that its material will be understandable to those with no formal theological training. Teaching God's truth to such is my life's work.

My wife, Nelun, and our children, Nirmali and Asiri, prayed this book through to its completion. Nelun's conviction that there was a need for a book on hell helped me to persevere in this project. I could never do the study and writing I do if my colleagues in Youth for Christ did not release me for this ministry. I am particularly grateful to Tony Senewiratne who took on the extra load of directing the work during my sabbatical and to his wife, Cal, who supported him through those busy months. I'm also thankful to relatives and friends in Sri Lanka and abroad who opened their homes for me to "hide" from my busy ministry activities and write.

This book is dedicated to my parents. My mother, who led me to Christ, was the first and most influential Bible teacher in my life. My father helped his children inherit a love for books and placed before us a model of commitment to hard work and Christian excellence. This book is a small tribute from a busy son who has received so much from them and given so little in return.

Nothing helped me persevere in writing a book on such a difficult topic as the perspective of the grace of God, given so richly to undeserving sinners. I hope that this book will give its readers a deeper appreciation of the marvels of grace and lead them to a firmer commitment to proclaim the message of grace to those who are lost and headed for eternal judgment.

PART ONE

BIBLICAL
AND
THEOLOGICAL
ISSUES

CHAPTER ONE

THE DECLINE OF HELL[1]

Christians have often told me that they can't remember the last time they heard a sermon about hell. American theologian Donald Bloesch has said, "If anything has disappeared from modern thought, it is the belief in a supernatural heaven and hell."[2] In 1986 only 23 percent of Europeans claimed to believe in hell.

A HISTORICAL PERSPECTIVE

There is a long history behind this disappearance of hell. One of the first big shifts in Christian thinking about hell occurred at the turn of the third century in the Egyptian city of Alexandria. A famous Christian teacher there, Clement of Alexandria, taught that God's purifying discipline of humanity extends beyond this life.

Clement's student, Origen, became even more influential than his teacher. He had problems with the concepts of damnation and the wrath of God. Using his famous allegorical method of interpreting Scripture, he rationalized the biblical references to punishment and ended up believing that punishment is a blessing from God. Hell became a place where the unrighteous will be disciplined. Eventually everyone will repent and be saved. This is the doctrine of universalism.

An influential fourth-century theologian, Gregory of Nyssa, also taught universalism, and by the fifth century it was widespread in the church. It was condemned as heretical by the second council of Constantinople in 553 A.D. As this council represented the whole church of its day, this condemnation effectively checked its spread.

In the period that followed, known as the Middle Ages, universalism emerged only rarely. The most famous universalist of this period was ninth-century Irish philosopher John Scotus Erigena. The period just before and after the sixteenth-century Protestant Reformation was a time of great intellectual ferment in the West. Yet universalism was not influential in the church. It seemed to have been found only in the fringes of the Anabaptist movement.

In the nineteenth and twentieth centuries the scene changed immensely. A key figure in this change was the German theologian Friedrich Schleiermacher (1768—1834), who has been called the father of modern theology. He held to a strong view of predestination, but refused to restrict this predestination to only some individuals. He believed that, given the unity of the human race, it is unlikely that God would treat some people differently than others and hoped for universal salvation.

By the beginning of the nineteenth century many people kept universalism as a private hope. Some, however, proclaimed it as a clear doctrine. In America, John Murray (1741—1815) founded the Universalist denomination that held universalism as a basic dogma. He and Hosea Ballou (1771—1852) wrote extensively in its defense. This denomination later joined the Unitarians to form the Unitarian-Universalist Church.

THE SITUATION TODAY

Universalism is a widespread doctrine today. It takes different forms, and its advocates argue for it in different ways. Some say the Scriptures teach, or at least imply, it. Respected biblical scholars like

C. H. Dodd of England and Ethelbert Stauffer of Germany, who were relatively orthodox in their approach to the Scriptures, held that Paul taught a universal homecoming at the end of time when all humanity will turn to God for salvation. The beloved Scottish Bible commentator William Barclay claimed to be a convinced universalist in his spiritual autobiography, which was published shortly before his death. He based his case partly on what he considered to be the biblical understanding of punishment as being remedial and temporary.

Others, like John A. T. Robinson and John Hick of England and Nels Ferre of America, approached the issue from a more theological or philosophical base. We can summarize this approach to punishment by saying that some think God is too good to send people to an eternal hell, while others think that humanity is too good or significant to be condemned in this way.

Some argue that because Christ came to save the world, everyone in the world should be saved. This was the direction in which the Swiss theologian Karl Barth moved. Though Barth himself remained agnostic about universalism, others followed this line of thinking and claimed that all are saved because of what Christ did, though all may not experience the benefits of salvation in this life.

Many today, like Barth, have chosen to be agnostic over the issue, saying that they do not know the answer to the question of whether all will be saved in the end. Different reasons are given for this agnosticism. Karl Barth said that God is sovereign and we mortals cannot, and must not, decide on what God will do in the end. The British biblical scholar C. Ryder Smith said that in the Bible there are two traditions about the final destiny of humanity. One speaks of eternal punishment and the other of universal restoration. As these are kept in unresolved tension in the Bible, we too must keep them in tension without being dogmatic one way or the other.

Many in the church today have universalism simply as a hope. Though they may not preach it dogmatically, they don't eliminate the possibility that all will be saved in the end. We may call them the "wishful universalists."

I have been told numerous times that there are many "closet universalists" in evangelical churches today. These are people who believe that all will be saved, but are afraid of being public about this belief as it is considered a heresy in orthodox Christian circles, and also because the idea that all will be saved could add to the spiritual apathy that characterizes this generation.

Related to the above position is that of evangelicals who are ashamed of hell. They are bound to believe everything that the Bible explicitly teaches, so they believe in an eternal hell. But they wish that they did not have to believe it. If they speak about the topic, which is not very often, they do so with a sense of shame, as if it were something very unjust, and they keep saying that they wish it were not true.

Another recent development in evangelical circles has been the growing popularity of *annihilationism*. Annihilationists believe that the punishment of the lost is a destruction resulting in the person ceasing to exist. The Adventist groups and cults like the Jehovah's Witnesses have long held a similar view, called conditional immortality, as one of their basic tenets.

THE CULTURAL UNACCEPTABILITY OF HELL

For many reasons hell has become culturally alien to the thinking of most people in modern society.

This is the age of *pluralism*. Pluralism affirms that differing viewpoints must be allowed to exist side by side. Its aim is to unite people who differ. The doctrine of hell, on the other hand, proclaims an irreversible division of humanity into two groups, the saved and the lost.

The rise of pluralism in this generation was perhaps inevitable. In the age of slavery and colonialism one group of people regarded themselves as superior to another. Many conservative Christians, who considered themselves guardians of orthodoxy, subscribed to the heresy of racial superiority. I still find myself cringing as I hear some of my fellow evangelicals speaking with the type of prejudice one would not have dreamed possible at the end of the twentieth century. Sensitive Christians find such prejudicial thinking abhorrent. The doctrine of hell reminds them of this unjust, discriminatory thinking.

If people who are embarrassed in this way are not committed to a doctrine of Scripture that requires them to believe every statement in it, then it would be easy for them to jettison the doctrine of hell along with the doctrine of racial superiority.

This is also the age of the *human potential movement*. Even preachers have been influenced by this. They preach that people are good and important and capable of great possibilities if only they would think positive thoughts about themselves. In such an environment it would seem out of place to tell people they are so sinful that unless they repent and turn to God they are doomed to eternal punishment. That would be like throwing a wet blanket onto a party celebrating the beauty of humanity!

This is also a *"feel good"* generation. Talk about hell does not make people feel good. Therefore, a lot of preachers have chosen to avoid talking about it. They are afraid that if they mention such unpleasant topics, some people will stop coming to their churches. Thus they emphasize only the love of God and what he can do in the lives of those who come to him. A popular evangelical preacher was asked, on television, why he condemns a certain sin. His response was that he does not condemn sin in his preaching. He preaches about the love of God, and not about sin and hell and such negative topics.

Then today we are seeing the *growth of eastern religious thinking* not only in the East, but also in the West. In the West, Buddhism and Hinduism, and especially "the New Age movements"—which have been influenced by Buddhism and Hinduism—are rapidly gaining popularity. These religions teach reincarnation, which provides many with an alternative to the "unpleasant" doctrine of hell.

Harvard Divinity School theologian Gordon Kaufman, after tracing four centuries of decline in the concepts of heaven and hell, says that what is left is intellectually empty baggage. He declares, "It seems to me we've gone through irreversible changes. I don"t think there can be any future for heaven and hell."[3]

So it is not surprising that hell is not a popular topic today. Based on his conversations over a number of years with evangelical theologians, Peter Toon asserts that "in conservative circles there is a seeming reluctance to espouse publicly a doctrine of hell, and where it is held there is a seeming tendency towards a doctrine of hell as annihilation."[4]

In this environment of hostility, confusion, and silence over the issue, Christians have questions about hell for which many are not able or willing to give adequate answers. This book is an attempt to remedy that situation.

CHAPTER TWO

WHAT WILL HELL BE LIKE?

I have a friend who was once active in church life, but who later rejected the gospel and lived with scant respect for God and his principles. I often talked to him about Christ. But he was not interested. One day I warned him that if he did not repent, he would go to hell. He laughed and said that he would be a stranger in heaven and that hell is where he would like to go. His friends will be in hell, and they could get together and have a nice time there. My friend had, or pretended to have, an idea of hell that made it an attractive place to be in.

A popular American comedian wrote a letter which was not to be opened until after he died. It was a letter that attacked Christian beliefs, especially the belief in the hereafter. It was published in a newspaper the day after his death in 1944. In it he says, "If one may judge by the people who are surest of going there, [heaven] must be a powerfully dull place, populated to a considerable and uncomfortable degree by prigs, time servers and unpleasantly aggressive individuals." His view of hell was much more pleasant: "Hell may have a worse climate, but undoubtedly the company is sprightlier."

What will hell be like? The Bible is not concerned to give precise details about its location and geography or about what people will be doing there. It tells us more about the occupation of those in heaven than about those in hell. The main reason for the biblical teaching about hell is to warn us about the dire consequences of sin and to encourage us along the path of repentance and perseverance in righteousness. Yet the Bible tells enough about hell to inform us that it will be a place of torment.

A PLACE

The various descriptions of hell always refer to it as a place. These are figurative descriptions and thus must not be interpreted with exact literalness. Hell belongs to the realm of eternity which is beyond time and space. Yet when the Bible speaks about hell, it uses imagery connected with a place. Because of our limited knowledge of eternity, we don't know what type of place this is. However, we know that it is indeed the equivalent of what in this life is known as "a place."

The Bible uses some graphic words to identify hell. The best known is the Greek word *gehenna*, which is usually translated "hell." This was the word Christ generally used for the place of punishment.[1] *Gehenna* is a transliteration of an Old Testament expression, "valley of Hinnom," which is a ravine on the south side of Jerusalem. In Israel's disobedient past this valley had been the center of idolatrous worship. Children had been burned there as an offering to the god Molech (2 Chron. 28:3; 33:6; Jer. 32:35). Jeremiah calls it "the Valley of Slaughter" because people were going to be killed there as part of God's judgment (Jer. 7:31-34). It later became the rubbish dump of Jerusalem. A fire consuming rubbish burned continually in this valley. So its history made it an appropriate place from which to derive a name for the place of eternal punishment, which is often described as a place with fires of torment.

Hell is described in the book of Revelation as the "fiery lake of burning sulfur" (19:20; see also 14:11; 20:10; 21:8) or simply as "the lake of fire" (20:14, 15). The figure of burning sulfur was used for volcanic eruptions. It was first used in the Bible in Genesis 19:24, which says that "the Lord rained down burning sulfur on Sodom and Gomorrah." Since then it has become a common symbol of divine judgment.

The Greek word *hades* usually refers to the abode of the dead—both righteous and unrighteous. Its Hebrew equivalent is *sheol*. Sometimes the NIV simply translates it as "grave" (Acts 2:27, 31). Sometimes it is translated as "death" (1 Cor. 15:55). In the story of Lazarus and the rich man the NIV translates *hades* as "hell," because here it is used to describe the place of the torment of the wicked: "In hell, where he was in torment . . ." (Luke 16:23).

The Greek words *tartaros*, meaning the underworld (2 Pet. 2:4), and *abussos*, meaning the abyss or bottomless pit (Rom. 10:7; Rev. 11:7; 17:8; 20:3), are used to describe abodes of the dead, of angels and demons, etc. They are not significant for our study, as they are temporary abodes.

A PLACE OF PUNISHMENT

Hell is essentially a place of punishment. The Bible teaches that this punishment is something terrible. It is terrible because the one who punishes is God. It involves exposure to the wrath of the pure and almighty God. We are told that "our God is a consuming fire" (Heb. 12:29). Therefore "it is a dreadful thing to fall into the hands of the living God" (Heb. 10:31). This latter statement comes from a passage describing "a fearful expectation of judgment and of raging fire that will consume the enemies of God" (Heb. 10:27). After mentioning the death penalty for lawbreakers prescribed in the Mosaic law, it says, "How much more severely do you think a man deserves to be punished who has trampled the Son of God under foot?" (10:29).

Romans 9:22 speaks of some people as "objects [literally, vessels] of [God's] wrath—prepared for destruction." Romans 2:5 says, "Because of your stubbornness and your unrepentant heart, you are storing up wrath against yourself for the day of God's wrath, when his righteous judgment will be revealed." Twice Paul says that "God's wrath comes on those who are disobedient" (Eph. 5:6; Col. 3:6).

Second Thessalonians 1:8, 9 places the focus directly on the idea of punishment: "He will punish those who do not know God and do not obey the gospel of our Lord Jesus. They will be punished with everlasting destruction and shut out from the presence of the Lord and from the majesty of his power."

This simple listing of texts should impress upon the reader the seriousness of the future judgment. One of the purposes of this book is to help its readers to realize this seriousness, so that it will influence their lives and ministries—especially their compassion for the lost.

A PLACE OF SEPARATION

The punishment of hell is essentially separation from God. In this life too the lost are separated from God. Paul says, "Remember that at that time you were separate from Christ, excluded from citizenship in Israel and foreigners to the covenants of the promise, without hope and without God in the world" (Eph. 2:12).

Though this is a very bleak picture, many sinners would not agree that theirs is a bleak life. They have been able to construct for themselves a life which, they claim, satisfies them. There is much self-deception here, for only the Creator of life can give a truly fulfilling life. But sinners are able to get an element of enjoyment out of life because they can use natural resources to have pleasurable experiences. Many wicked people are wealthy, and there are a lot of things that money can buy on earth.

The Bible affirms that on earth the unrighteous experience some of God's blessings. Jesus said that God "causes his sun to rise on the evil and the good, and sends rain on the righteous and the unrighteous" (Matt. 5:45). Paul told the people in Lystra that God "has shown kindness by giving you rain from heaven and crops in their seasons; he provides you with plenty of food and fills your hearts with joy" (Acts 14:17). These blessings are not the same as salvation. Until one receives God's salvation, he or she is "without God in the world," as Ephesians 2:12 stated.

So we have a paradox. People without God experience many of God's blessings. John says that Christ, "the true light . . . gives light to every man" (John 1:9). But Paul says that without him people are "darkness" (Eph. 5:8). Salvation means being "called . . . out of darkness into his wonderful light" (1 Pet. 2:9). Paul told the people of Athens that in God all people "live and move and have [their] being" (Acts 17:28). Yet in Romans 6:23 he says that "the wages of sin is death" and implies that all who are outside of Christ are dead. Jesus said, "Whoever hears my word and believes him who sent me has eternal life . . . he has crossed over from death to life" (John 5:24).

What do we make of these paradoxes? They mean that while sinners do not have salvation, they enjoy some blessings that come from God, who is the sustainer of creation. While sinners are spiritually dead and miss "life . . . to the full" (John 10:10), they still have a life in which each aspect of their personalities has some expression. While they walk in darkness not knowing God, they still have some light which is derived from God. A sinner could use this light to excel in art or science or to have pleasurable experiences.

At the judgment the unbeliever's separation from God is consummated. There those vestiges of contact with God which he had on earth are destroyed. He will hear God say, "I don't know you or where you come from. Away from me, all you evildoers!" (Luke 13:27). This is "the second death" (Rev. 20:14; 21:8). On earth he had some light, though walking in darkness, but at the judgment he is cast into "outer darkness" (Matt. 8:12; 22:13, RSV).

Everything good about the humanity of the unrepentant will be stripped off at the judgment. The Creator, who sustained his creation, will let go of this hold, and the blessings of life and humanity which the person had taken for granted will be taken away from him. No wonder Jesus said of Judas, "It would be better for him if he had not been born" (Matt. 26:24). There is nothing good that survives the judgment of the lost.

A PLACE OF CONSCIOUS TORMENT

Does the loss of all the blessings of humanity at the judgment mean that after that the person ceases to exist? Some have thought so. Yet the Bible teaches that the dehumanized state of the lost is a conscious state.

Torment

Though the word "torment" does not sound appropriate to modern sensitivities, it is used twice in Revelation to describe the suffering of those individuals who serve the Antichrist (Rev. 14:10, 11) and once to describe the suffering of Satan, the Antichrist, and his prophet (Rev. 20:10). The related noun is used twice in the story of Lazarus and the rich man to describe the suffering of hell (Luke 16:23, 28).

These related Greek words (the verb *basanizō* and nouns *basanos*, *basanismos* and *basanistēs*) appear over twenty times in the New Testament. They are, as we saw, used five times to refer to the future punishment. An examination of the way they are used shows that each time conscious torment is meant. The *Greek-*

English Lexicon by Bauer, Arndt, Gingrich, and Danker lists three ways in which the verb is used. It can be used literally of the torture in judicial examination, figuratively of any severe distress, or generally of harassing. In each case conscious torment is intended.[2] The contexts in which they appear bear this out.

The first appearance of the verb in the New Testament is representative of the rest. In Matthew 8:6, a Roman centurion tells Jesus, "Lord, my servant lies at home paralyzed and in terrible suffering." The verb (used here as a participle) is translated as "in . . . suffering" and describes severe distress. So the word is used often for the anguish associated with physical suffering.

It can also be used to mean torture. Revelation 9:5 says, "They were not given power to kill them, but only to *torture* them for five months. And the *agony* they suffered was like that of the sting of a scorpion when it strikes a man." The Greek verb and noun appear three times in this verse, though the NIV shows only two words: "torture" and "agony."

This evidence of the use of the related Greek words for "torment" leads us to expect the torment of the lost mentioned in Revelation 14:11 to mean conscious suffering. This is confirmed from the context in which it appears:

> A third angel followed them and said in a loud voice: "If anyone worships the beast and his image . . . he too will drink of the wine of God's fury, which has been poured full strength into the cup of his wrath. He will be *tormented* with burning sulfur in the presence of the holy angels and of the Lamb. And the smoke of their *torment* rises for ever and ever. There is no rest day or night for those who worship the beast and his image. . . ." (Rev. 14:9-11)

Note that the punishment described here is both conscious and eternal.

In the story of Lazarus and the rich man, the related verb

(*basanos*) is used to describe the suffering of the rich man. The NIV translates it as "in torment": "In hell, where he was in torment . . . he called to [Abraham]" (Luke 16:23; see also verse 28). The next verse uses another word (*odunaomai*) which also carries the idea of conscious torment: "I am in agony in this fire." In both these verses we must conclude that conscious torment is intended.

Weeping and Gnashing of Teeth

In three of the parables about the Kingdom, Jesus says that those excluded from the Kingdom are sent to a place where there will be "weeping" and "gnashing of teeth" (Matt. 13:42, 50; 22:13). He uses the same expression in a non-parabolic discourse too: "But the subjects of the kingdom will be thrown outside, into the darkness, where there will be weeping and gnashing of teeth" (Matt. 8:12). Though these are figurative statements, the figures are intended to describe conscious suffering.

A PLACE OF REGRET

The future punishment is one of conscious torment; hence hell is a place of deep regret over decisions made on earth. Jesus talks about this regret vividly in the story of Lazarus and the rich man (Luke 16:23-30).

Those who rejected Christ will encounter him as a sovereign Judge. Their rebellion against God has been overthrown. They will be forced to join in the great affirmation when "at the name of Jesus every knee should bow, in heaven and on earth and under the earth, and every tongue confess that Jesus Christ is Lord" (Phil. 2:10, 11). The saved will do so joyously, while the lost do so with fear (on this, see Chapter 6). The old self-confidence is gone. Now they look at Christ as the vanquished look at the victor.

So my friend and the comedian were greatly mistaken when they dismissed the threat of hell with the humorous claims that they will be happy there. Their friends may indeed be there. But they will then be devoid of those gifts of humanity that make people capable of enjoying friendship. Yet in hell people will have enough of their humanness to regret their rejection of God on earth. On the other hand, the people whom the comedian found distasteful would lose their unpleasantness when they get to heaven, which will be a place of entirely pleasant, personal relationships.

DEGREES OF PUNISHMENT

Everyone in hell will not receive the same intensity of punishment. The idea that there will be degrees of punishment in hell may sound strange to many who have grown up believing that it is dangerous to differentiate between big and small sins. They have been taught that those who commit "big" and "small" sins are sinners equally in need of salvation. Many have extended this understanding of sin to their understanding of judgment and have concluded that everyone who is lost goes to the same hell and will face the same punishment.

Indeed all people are sinners and have no hope of salvation however good their lives may have been by earthly standards. All the lost, as far as we know, will go to the same hell. But the Bible also teaches that the sinfulness of some people is more serious than that of others, and that those whose sinfulness is more serious are headed for a more serious punishment. There are many places in Scripture where this is either taught or implied.

Judgment According to Light Received

Matthew 11:20-24 says that though Tyre, Sidon, and Sodom were destroyed for their wickedness, they had not received as much light as Korazin, Bethsaida, and Capernaum, which had witnessed Christ's miracles. At the judgment it would be more bearable for the wicked cities of Tyre, Sidon, and Sodom than it would be for the other cities, even though from a purely human perspective they seemed to be less wicked than the former. The principle is that those who have received more light have a greater degree of responsibility and so face a more severe punishment.

Luke 12:47, 48 is even more explicit. Jesus says, "The servant who knows his master's will and does not get ready [for his coming] or does not do what his master wants will be beaten with many blows." This servant had a lot of light but disregarded it. On the other hand, "The one who does not know and does things deserving punishment will be beaten with a few blows." He had enough light to be held accountable for his actions, so he was punished. But because the master's will had not been explicitly communicated to him, he received a few blows. Next Jesus gives the principle behind this reasoning: "From everyone who has been given much, much will be demanded; and from the one who has been entrusted with much, much more will be asked."

Hebrews 10:26-29 describes the punishment afforded to those who reject the gospel after understanding its contents:

> If we deliberately keep on sinning after we have received the knowledge of the truth, no sacrifice for sins is left, but the fearful expectation of judgment and of raging fire that will consume the enemies of God. Anyone who rejected the law of Moses died without mercy on the testimony of two or three witnesses. How much more severely do you think a man deserves to be punished who has trampled the Son of God under foot . . . ?

Judgment of Works

The Bible also teaches that the actions of people will be taken into account at the judgment. Revelation 20:12, 13 says that after the "books were opened . . . the dead were judged according to what they had done as recorded in the books." This may be called the judgment of works. People cannot be saved by works (Eph. 2:9). But their works are not immune to the judgment. Ecclesiastes 12:14 says, "God will bring every deed into judgment, including every hidden thing, whether it is good or evil."

Elsewhere the Scriptures say that the sins that have been confessed and forgiven are forgotten by God (Jer. 31:34). We can be assured that these are exempt from the judgment. But all other deeds, whether good or bad, will be brought before the judgment.

So in hell everyone will not suffer to the same extent. But we do not know in what ways this suffering will be different.

CHAPTER THREE

WHAT ABOUT ANNIHILATIONISM?

"Fire, then nothing." That succinctly describes the annihilationist approach to the final destiny of the lost. According to this view, the punishment upon the lost is eternal, in that it is irrevocable. The fires of judgment consume the sinner and he is destroyed, so that after this destruction, no person exists.

Just as universalism is gaining ground in the more liberal segments of the church, annihilationism is gaining ground in the more conservative segments of the church today. Some recent respected evangelical dictionaries and doctrinal books have cautiously presented annihilationism as one of two possible options for evangelical belief, the other being the traditional view of conscious, everlasting punishment.[1]

THE SUFFERING GOES ON FOREVER

The discussion on conscious torment in the last chapter would have already presented a strong case against annihilationism. The annihilationist may, however, say that the torment spoken of in the

Scriptures is temporary. It takes place at the time that the fires consume the person being punished.

However, there are texts in the Bible that teach that the suffering of hell goes on forever. Revelation 14:11, describing the punishment of followers of the Antichrist, says, ". . . the smoke of their torment rises for ever and ever." This seems to indicate that the torment is eternal. The annihilationist may present the very unlikely interpretation that though the smoke of the torment rises forever, the torment itself does not last forever. That interpretation is eliminated in the second part of this verse, which says, "There is no rest day and night for those who worship the beast. . . ." This implies that the lost are awake day and night. As this comes immediately after the words "for ever and ever," we can conclude that this statement teaches that the lost have "no rest day and night" for eternity.

Mark 9:43-48 also associates the suffering of the lost with eternity. Here Jesus says that the danger of hell is so serious that it would be better to suffer great deprivation on earth, such as getting rid of the hand or the foot or the eye, if that helps one to avoid the much greater suffering of hell. Jesus uses the word *gehenna* three times in this passage. We have already said that this word comes from the "Valley of Hinnom," the city dump of Jerusalem where a fire burned all the time. Jesus would have been thinking of this when he went on to say about *gehenna* that "their worm does not die, and the fire is not quenched." His point is that the suffering of hell goes on and on. Just as in the Valley of Hinnom the fire is not quenched and the worm does not die, so in *gehenna* the forces of destruction will go on and on acting on the lost.

The thrust of this passage may be summarized thus: hell is a place where the fire goes on and on. So it is worth depriving yourself of a hand, a foot, or an eye if by doing so you can go to heaven, because those are temporary deprivations, whereas the torment of hell is eternal.

EXAMINING THE "BIBLICAL" CASE FOR ANNIHILATIONISM

The above texts teach that the torment of the lost is conscious and eternal. However, the annihilationists appeal to another body of Scripture which, they say, teaches annihilation. In fact, some accuse those holding to the traditional view of "exegetical flimsiness."[2] We will now briefly examine the "biblical evidence" for annihilationism.

The Fires of Judgment

Fire is often used in the Bible to describe the nature of judgment. Annihilationists say that the main function of fire is not to cause pain but to secure destruction. We agree. But it also causes pain. So the question we must ask is, what did the biblical writers intend their readers to understand when they described punishment using the imagery of fire?

Annihilationists agree that because we have experienced the acute pain of being burned, fire is usually associated in our minds with conscious torment.[3] However, they say this is not the main function of fire. While that is true, we must remember that the Bible is not a technical science book. When the writers used some imagery to illustrate a truth, they usually used it in the sense that the people who read it would understand it. Technically the main function of fire may be to destroy. But when people think of fire in connection with punishment, what usually comes to their mind is the pain of being burned. So it is most likely that the biblical writers used it in this sense.

The Jewish writers of the inter-testamental period used fire in the sense of torment when referring to punishment. The second-century B.C. book of Judith, which is part of the Old Testament Apocrypha, says, "Woe to the nations that rise up against my people! The Lord Almighty will take vengeance on them in the day of judgment, fire and worms he will give to their flesh; and they shall weep in pain for ever" (16:17, RSV). The Fourth Book of Maccabees, which also comes from the second century B.C., says, "Because of this, justice has laid up for you intense and eternal fire and tortures, and these throughout all time will never let you go" (12:12, RSV).

These inter-testamental writings are not a suitable base for doctrine. But they show that Jews were accustomed to using the imagery of fire to describe torment. So it is very possible that when the New Testament authors used fire to describe judgment, they too meant torment.

The deciding factor when determining the meaning of picture language used in a passage is the context of the occurrence. Contextual evidence abounds for the use of fire to describe conscious suffering. This is the case with the rich man in the story of Lazarus. He says, "I am in agony in this fire" (Luke 16:24). Revelation 14:9-11 says, "If anyone worships the beast and his image . . . he will be tormented with burning sulfur in the presence of the holy angels and of the Lamb. And the smoke of their torment rises for ever and ever." "Burning sulfur" is a paraphrase for what is literally, "fire and sulfur." Revelation 20:10 says, "And the devil, who deceived them, was thrown into the lake of burning sulfur [literally, fire and sulfur], where the beast and the false prophet had been thrown. They will be tormented day and night for ever and ever." These are cases where the figure of fire is used to describe conscious torment.

It has been objected that in the last passage cited, those being tormented (the beast and the false prophet) are not individual people but symbols of the world in its hostility to God. Symbols, of course, cannot experience pain.[4] Even if the interpretation that personalities are not meant is correct, that does not eliminate Satan (Rev. 20:10) and those who worship the beast (Rev. 14:9-11), who are said to suffer torment from fire. Definite personalities are meant in these instances.

The above reasoning shows that annihilation is not intended by the biblical use of fire.

Judgment as Destruction

Annihilationists say that the word "destroy," which is used often to describe punishment, should be taken to mean what it literally means. If that were so, then the destroyed person would cease to exist. But we know that much of the vocabulary describing judgment is figurative. Could not "destroy" also be used figuratively? We speak of the alcoholic who has destroyed his life. That does not mean he ceases to exist. It means that his alcoholism has deprived him of those things about life that are good and beautiful. This is the type of thing the destruction of judgment does to those who are condemned. It destroys from their existence everything that is good and beautiful. Nothing remains that is worthy of the word "life."

Also, the particular word for "destroy" (*apollumi*) that the annihilationists appeal to is used sometimes with the meaning of "lose." Jesus warned us to "be afraid of the one who can destroy (*apolesai*) both soul and body in hell" (Matt. 10:28). Here is a use of the word "destroy" in the context of punishment. But earlier in the same discourse this same Greek word is used with the meaning of "lose." Jesus tells his disciples in Matthew 10:6, "Go rather to the lost (*apolōlota*) sheep of Israel." In the parables of the lost sheep, the lost coin, and the lost son, the word used for "lost" is this same word, *apollumi* (Luke 15:4, 6, 8, 9, 24, 32). These objects of affection were not annihilated—they were lost.

We conclude that when the word "destroy" is used in connection with judgment, it takes meanings other than the cessation of existence. This is buttressed by the fact that the same authors who use the idea of destroy to describe judgment also describe judgment in ways that must be understood as meaning conscious suffering, as we have shown earlier. As Jonathan Edwards has said, the death worthy of the name destruction is a conscious death.

The Opposite of Eternal Life

The Bible often describes the reward of salvation in terms of eternal life. The opposite of this is eternal death. Death to us usually means the cessation of existence. Therefore annihilationists claim that eternal death also means the cessation of existence.

Yet death is used often in a metaphorical sense when referring to the state of the lost. There are some people who are physically alive who are described as being dead. Paul describes the pre-conversion state as death through trespasses and sins (Eph. 2:1, 5; see also Col. 2:13). He says that "the widow who lives for pleasure is dead even while she lives" (1 Tim. 5:6). The Gospels describe the coming of Jesus as the dawning of a light to those who sat in the region of the shadow of death (Matt. 4:16; Luke 1:79; see also Isa. 9:2). These statements describe the state of the living lost as one of spiritual death.

The meaning of eternal death is illustrated from the meaning of its converse—eternal life. The essential idea of eternal life in the Bible is not existence as opposed to nonexistence, but life belonging to the age to come. Those who have eternal life have the blessings of the Kingdom of Heaven. They have "life . . . to the full" (John 10:10). The converse—eternal death—should mean an existence devoid of these blessings of the age to come.

Leon Morris's description of spiritual death explains this well:

> Death is not simply an event, it is a state, it is the sphere in which evil has its sway, and sinners are, and must be, within this sphere with all that that means until they are redeemed from it. If a man continues in sin, he continues in death.[5]

After the judgment this state of death is intensified, and the unrepentant experience what is known as "the second death" (Rev. 2:11; 20:6, 14; 21:8).

Immortality of the Soul

Annihilationists often say that our belief in an everlasting existence of the lost comes from a belief in the immortality of the soul, which, they say, is a concept taken over from Greek thought rather than the Bible. We agree that many Christians have an unbiblical view of the soul that has been influenced by Greek dualism, which draws too much of a distinction between the soul and the body.

In the next life there is going to be a resurrection of the body. What was wrong with the Greek conception was the dualistic separation of the body and the soul as opposed to the wholistic biblical view that conceives of the human being as a unity. If some people obtained their view of the unending existence of persons from the Greek view of human nature, then they have got it from an erroneous source. But they don't need to discard this belief, for the Bible also teaches it.

A Marred Heaven?

The annihilationist argument that heaven cannot be a place of bliss as long as there are people in hell is discussed in Chapter 6.

ANNIHILATION AND *NIRVANA*

Annihilation is very similar to what orthodox Buddhists view as salvation. In the Buddhist scheme the devotee achieves *Nirvana* after a long climb representing numerous rebirths. The *Nirvana* of orthodox Buddhism is quite similar to the annihilation we are responding to here. What to the Buddhist is a reward after climbing a difficult path is similar to the punishment for sin in the eyes of the annihilationist! This has prompted someone to speak of the "bliss of annihilation."

We will show in Chapter 12 that the prospect of hell is a key source of motivation to repentance. If the hell we present to a Buddhist is something close to their blissful goal of *Nirvana*, then they would see no need to turn to Christ. Thus annihilationism could become a major hindrance to evangelism. Having spent all my life in ministry working with Buddhists, I know how hard it is for them to make their final decision to break with the religion of their people in order to follow Christ. Many who are convinced of the truth about Jesus are yet reluctant to commit themselves to him because of the costliness of such a step. Why should such a person bother to pay this price if the consequence of rejecting Christ is so similar to their goal of *Nirvana*?

CHAPTER FOUR

HOW LONG WILL HELL LAST?

There are many in the church who, while accepting the fact that there will be a hell, say that it will not last forever. This was what the early church father Origen believed.

In the "high church" traditions of the Anglican communion and in the Roman Catholic Church, there has long been a belief in a purgatory. So they have prayers for the dead as part of their ritual. These prayers, however, were for professing Christians in purgatory who are en route to heaven. Now this hope is being extended in some circles to all people.

THE MEANING OF ETERNAL

William Barclay, in arguing for a temporary punishment, says that the Greek words used for "eternal" in the Bible do not necessarily mean everlasting.[1] The noun *aion*, which is translated "ever" and "eternal," originally meant "an age." The adjective, *aionios*, translated "eternal," originally meant "belonging to the age." So the word *eternal* is often used to refer to the quality of the age rather than the duration of the age. With this we agree. But this is not always the case. Often these words take on the idea of duration rather than, or along with, the idea of quality.

Hebrews 13:8 says that "Jesus Christ is the same yesterday and today and forever (*aiōnas*)." Clearly the word is used in a temporal sense here. The verse is saying that Jesus is everlastingly the same.

Sometimes this idea is expressed with even more stress by repeating the word "ever." Revelation 4:10 and 10:6 say that God lives "for ever and ever." Revelation 11:15 says, "He will reign for ever and ever." It would be unnatural to take "ever and ever" in these statements as meaning anything other than "everlasting." The phrase "ever and ever" is used in Revelation for eternal punishment too: "The smoke of their torment rises for ever and ever" (Rev. 14:11); "They will be tormented day and night for ever and ever" (Rev. 20:10). Here too the words must mean everlasting.

Rene Pache reminds us that the word "eternal" is used sixty-four times to refer to "the divine and blessed realities of the other world." He says, "In all these cases, it is beyond all doubt a question of duration without end."[2] This same word is used a few times to refer to eternal punishment, which is the antithesis of these blessings. Is it not logical to conclude that in these cases also it should mean duration without end?

The universalist Nels Ferre concedes that "the Christian message brought forth a concept of eternity as duration correlative to its understanding of God." He says that eternal life means "both a quality of life which God is and gives and the quantity which he bestows which is as long as his own faithfulness."[3] Eternal life and eternal death are corresponding opposites. They are mentioned together in Matthew 25:46: "Then they will go away to eternal punishment, but the righteous to eternal life." This is why Ferre cannot use the biblical concept of "eternal" in his case for universalism. He has to concede that the biblical writers meant everlasting when they referred to eternal punishment.

Another universalist, German New Testament scholar Ethelbert Stauffer, also agrees that the Bible teaches irreversible punishment. But he says that Paul, in his later epistles, came to believe that there will be "a universal homecoming" when all will be saved.[4] The fact that some universalists concede that the Bible teaches everlasting punishment is a strong argument against attempts to understand eternal punishment as a temporary state.

Mark 3:29 says, "Whoever blasphemes against the Holy Spirit will never be forgiven; he is guilty of an eternal sin." It is not immediately apparent whether the word "eternal" here is temporal or qualitative. But the parallel passage in Matthew shows that it is temporal. It says, ". . . will not be forgiven, either in this age or in the age to come" (Matt. 12:32). So "eternal" means forever here.

We must remember, as A. A. Hodge points out, that "the Greek language possesses no more emphatic terms with which to express the idea of endless duration" than these words which we are examining.[5] We conclude that when the Bible uses "eternal" to describe eternal life and eternal punishment, it means everlasting.

IS ETERNAL PUNISHMENT REMEDIAL?

William Barclay also claims that punishment in the Bible is always remedial and therefore eternal punishment should also be remedial.[6] We agree that the Bible speaks often of remedial punishment in this life. But when it describes punishment in the next life, it is as an irreversible state.

There are many passages in Scripture that teach that the punishment of hell is irreversible. We have already referred to the passages that say there is no forgiveness, in this life or the next, for the sin of blasphemy against the Holy Spirit (Matt. 12:32; Mark 3:29). When the Gospels describe hell, many of the figures used imply that its duration is everlasting. It is described as a place "where the fire never goes out" and "where 'their worm does not die'" (Mark 9:43, 48). Indeed this is figurative language, but the figures are intended to communicate the idea of endlessness.

The eternal separation of heaven from hell is implied in the story of the rich man and Lazarus. Abraham tells the rich man, "Between us and you a great chasm has been fixed, so that those who want to go from here to you cannot, nor can anyone cross over from there to us" (Luke 16:26). Some have objected to the use of this story, saying it is a parable and does not qualify as an accurate source of theology. Leon Morris agrees that "this is no doubt a pictorial detail," but he says that the picture is used to convey the meaning "that in the afterlife there is no passing from one state to the other." In fact, he points out that "the Greek implies that this is the purpose and not simply the result of the great chasm."[7]

Another objection to the use of this passage as evidence for an eternal hell is that the word translated "hell" that is used here is not *gehenna*, the usual word for hell, but *hades*, the word for the abode of the dead. We said in Chapter 2 that *hades* is used in different ways in the Bible. It is a general word for the place of the dead. We argue that the context, with its description of torment, indicates that here it is hell that is intended.

A comment of Jesus about Judas also implies that there would be no further chance for him. Jesus says, "It would be better for him if he had not been born" (Matt. 26:24). A. H. Strong says about this statement that "if at any time even after the lapse of ages, Judas be redeemed, his subsequent infinite duration of blessedness must outweigh all the finite sufferings through which he has passed."[8] If he would be saved someday, then it would have been good for him to be born.

TEXTS IMPLYING REPENTANCE IN HELL

The third biblical argument for a temporary hell is drawn from three texts that are said to teach that there will be an opportunity for people to repent in hell.

The most popularly used text is 1 Peter 3:19, 20 which says that Christ "went and preached to the spirits in prison who disobeyed long ago when God waited patiently in the days of Noah while the ark was being built." This preaching is said to imply that those in hell get an opportunity to hear the gospel.

Most of the standard contemporary commentaries on 1 Peter[9] accept the view that the spirits referred to here are probably not human beings. They point out that when the Greek word for spirit (*pneuma*) appears without any qualifying words before or after it, that refers to good or bad supernatural beings (see Matt. 12:45; Luke 10:20; Heb. 1:14). Peter is probably referring to the disobedient angels who married the sons and daughters of men and caused much harm to the human race. They are mentioned in Genesis 6:1-4, just before the Noah story; so Peter's association of them with the days of Noah is understandable. Peter is probably describing a proclamation of Christ's victory to the forces of darkness that buffet human beings. This fits in well with the context of the passage, which seeks to give encouragement to persecuted Christians.

More recently Wayne Grudem has argued that the preaching referred to here was done during the time of Noah to people who are now in prison or hell. According to this view, the preaching was done by Noah, who was acting as the spokesman of Christ.[10]

At least three other interpretations of this text have received prominence. One of them could be used to support a second chance theory. We would simply say that this is a highly disputed verse that seems to be speaking of preaching that was done to a specific group of people or spirits at a specific time. To use such a verse to build a doctrine of a second chance, which seems to go so much against the grain of the rest of Scripture, is a precarious enterprise that makes one dangerously susceptible to the error of misrepresenting the Word of God.

The next passage is 1 Peter 4:6 which says that "the gospel was preached even to those who are now dead." Some have claimed that this speaks of preaching to people after they died, giving them the possibility of a second chance of salvation. The weight of contemporary biblical scholarship is for taking "the dead" referred to here as Christians who have died during the persecution of the church. The gospel was preached to them *before* they died, and not after.

The second chance interpretation of this verse does not fit into its context. It is found in the middle of a passage that seeks to encourage Christians to persevere amidst persecution. As Wayne Grudem points out, "It would hardly encourage Peter's persecuted readers to persevere as Christians in the hard path of obedience if the easy road to debauchery could all be renounced and forgiven after they died."[11] Peter has just said (v. 5) that those who take the road of debauchery (described in vv. 3, 4) will be judged for their wickedness.[12]

The third text said to teach that there will be a chance to repent after death is 1 Corinthians 15:29: "Now if there is no resurrection, what will those do who are baptized for the dead? If the dead are not raised at all, why are people baptized for them?" It is claimed that if there is such a thing as baptism for the dead, then it means there is a chance of the fortunes of people changing after death.

This is the only time the practice of baptizing for the dead is mentioned in the Bible. The commentary of Archibald Robertson and Alfred Plummer says there have been thirty-six different explanations of what this practice is.[13] We are not told that Paul endorses the practice. In this passage Paul is combating the false teachers who said that there is no resurrection from the dead. They denied the reality of the afterlife. Paul seems to be pointing out their inconsistency here. They say there is no afterlife, but they still baptize for the dead! "Why do that," Paul is asking, "if you don't believe in an afterlife?"

These three difficult texts simply do not qualify to be used to construct a doctrine of salvation in hell.

THE FINALITY OF OUR CHOICES ON EARTH

The whole tenor of Scripture is in the direction of the finality of opportunity in this life. Hebrews 9:27 says, "Man is destined to die once, and after that to face judgment." Many times we are told, "Today" is the day of salvation (Heb. 3:7, 13, 15; 4:7). Isaiah wrote: "Seek the Lord while he may be found; call on him while he is near" (Isa. 55:6). The implication in these texts is that the day of opportunity will end.

The parable of the ten virgins ends with the foolish virgins clamoring to get in but being told, "I tell you the truth, I don't know you" (Matt. 25:12). They came after "the door was shut" (v. 10). After relating this story Jesus says, "Therefore keep watch, because you do not know the day or the hour" (v. 13). This parable implies that after the judgment there is no hope for people to enter the Kingdom, even if they desire to do so.

There are many instances of people who, after having received ample opportunity to see either the judgment or the grace of God, refused to repent of their chosen path of disobedience. Jesus explained this in the story of the rich man and Lazarus. The rich man asked Abraham to send Lazarus to preach to his five brothers. He felt that the miracle of a dead man coming to them would cause them to regard the message with some seriousness. Abraham's response is, "If they do not listen to Moses and the Prophets, they will not be convinced even if someone rises from the dead" (Luke 16:31).

The book of Revelation gives instances of people who go through some of the most terrible plagues and still refuse to repent. Revelation chapter 16 describes the seven bowls of God's wrath. Each one gets more and more difficult to bear. But twice we are told, "They refused to repent" (vv. 9, 11). The chapter ends with the words, "And they cursed God on account of the plague of hail, because the plague was so terrible" (v. 21). In Revelation 9, after a similar listing of plagues as in chapter 16, we are told, "The rest of mankind that were not killed by these plagues still did not repent of the work of their hands; they did not stop worshiping demons, and idols. . . . Nor did they repent of their murders, their magic arts, their sexual immorality or their thefts" (vv. 20, 21).

Universalists say that the torment of hell will cause the people to repent. The above passages show that there are some who refuse to leave their chosen path of rebellion, no matter how intense the influences are that are brought to bear on them.

Toward the end of the book of Revelation we find the words, "Let him who does wrong continue to do wrong; let him who is vile continue to be vile; let him who does right continue to do right; and let him who is holy continue to be holy" (22:11). This passage does not say that there is no chance of repentance for people who live on earth. The door of opportunity to repent will be open right until the end, as we are told a little later: "Whoever is thirsty, let him come; and whoever wishes, let him take the free gift of the water of life" (22:17). But this and the other passages discussed above show us that it is possible for people to remain permanently closed to the truth.

These texts are in keeping with the other body of texts that state that in the afterlife there is no more possibility of people repenting. They will by then have become set in their ways. Not even judgment will drive them to repentance.

CHAPTER FIVE

THE UNIVERSAL SAVIOR OF THE WORLD

When I was in my teens, on vacation in the mountains, we went to worship in the local church. It was Evangelism Sunday, and the preacher's sermon was on why we should preach the gospel. He said Christ has saved everyone in the world, but everyone still does not know that they are saved; evangelism is telling people that they have been saved and can now enjoy the benefits of this salvation.

The appeal to universalism from the idea that Christ is the Savior of the world is made using certain biblical texts and also through theological systems that emphasize the universality of Christ's work.

THE UNIVERSALISTIC TEXTS

There was a time when biblical texts were used extensively in support of the universalistic position. But this is not so today. Universalists say that what is important is not whether the Bible teaches universalism or not. Rather, it is the supposed fact that the Christian gospel does not make sense if hell is everlasting. For this reason I will deal with the so-called "universalistic texts" only very briefly.[1]

Christ's Salvation Is Universal in Its Availability

The first body of texts used by universalists are those that state that Christ's salvation is available to all the people in the world. These texts appear especially in the writings of John and Paul. Upon study we see that the contexts of these verses make it necessary to limit the salvation which these verses describe to those who believe in Christ. Sometimes belief as a condition for salvation is presented in the same paragraph as the "universalistic text." Thus the only way that we can take them as teaching universalism is to hold that John and Paul held two contrary views and proclaimed them at the same time. This would make them schizoid, like Dr. Jekyll and Mr. Hyde—a most unlikely situation!

John 3:16, probably the most popular gospel text, is used to support universalism. But it clearly states that though the salvation Christ gives is for the whole world, one must first believe in order to be saved and avoid perishing.

Second Corinthians 5:19a says, "God was reconciling the world to himself in Christ, not counting men's sins against them." Some universalists use this to say that every individual is already reconciled even though he or she may not experience the blessings of this reconciliation. If so, what Paul says next would not make sense: "He has committed to us the message of reconciliation" (v. 19b). Then he explains what that means: "We implore you on Christ's behalf: Be reconciled to God" (v. 20). Even though God's work in reconciling the world to himself in Christ is complete, individuals must be personally reconciled to God. There is a universal availability of salvation. But it has to be appropriated personally through faith.

John 1:29 says that Jesus is "the Lamb of God, who takes

away the sin of the world." But that same book also says, "I told you that you would die in your sins; if you do not believe that I am the one I claim to be, you will indeed die in your sins" (8:24). In his first epistle, John says that Jesus Christ is "the atoning sacrifice for our sins, and not only for ours but also for the sins of the whole world" (1 John 2:2) . But he later says, "Anyone who does not love remains in death. Anyone who hates his brother is a murderer, and you know that no murderer has eternal life in him" (3:14, 15).

The message conveyed by these "universalistic texts" is that Christ's salvation is universal in its offer.

The Use of the Word "All"

Verses that use the word "all" when describing the experience of salvation are also used by universalists. They take "all" here in the absolute sense of meaning every person who ever lived.

Before examining these texts we must point out that often in the Bible "all" cannot take the absolute sense. Mark 1:5 says that "the whole Judean countryside and all the people of Jerusalem went out to [John the Baptist]." It is obvious that this does not mean that every single person in Jerusalem went to hear him. "All" here refers to an unusually large number of people (see also Acts 9:35; 19:10).

N. T. Wright has pointed out that the word "all" can be used to refer to "all of some kinds" or "some of all kinds."[2] We will show that this is so with the "universalistic texts."

Salvation Is Available to All Types of People

One group of universalistic passages says that the salvation that Jesus brings is not confined to the Jews (as some of the Jewish believers in the early church taught), or to a spiritual elite (as the precursors of the Gnostics in the early church taught), but to all who would believe.

In John 12:32 Jesus says, "But I, when I am lifted up from the earth, will draw all men to myself." Some universalists have claimed that this statement teaches that Christ's death will result in the salvation of all people. That interpretation seems unlikely when we note that John has Jesus stating a few verses later, "There is a judge for the one who rejects me and does not accept my words; that very word which I spoke will condemn at the last day" (v. 48).

The context helps us understand what it means for Jesus to draw all men to himself. This discourse was sparked off by the announcement that some Greeks wanted to see Jesus (vv. 20-22). His response is to talk about his death and its effect of drawing all men to himself (vv. 23-33). A. T. Robertson points out that what Christ is saying is that "this is the way that Greeks can and will come to Christ, by way of the cross."[3] By his death he opened the door of salvation not only to the Jews but to people from all races, like these Greeks who wanted to see him.

This is the way we should understand 1 Timothy 4:10 also. Here Paul says that "God . . . is the Savior of all men, and especially of those who believe." In 1 Timothy, Paul was combating the false teachers who taught that salvation is available only to a spiritual elite (incipient Gnosticism). This is part of his answer to them.

Salvation Is for All Who Are in Christ

There are two texts that are popular with universalists, because the word "all" is used in parallel couplets where one use refers to everybody. The first of these is Romans 5:18 which says that "just as the result of one trespass [by Adam] was condemnation for all men, so also the result of one act of righteousness [by Christ] was justification that brings life for all men." Universalists say that because we must take the first of these statements as referring to every person, we must take the second statement also to refer to every person.

If the universalistic interpretation is true, we are left with the difficulty of trying to explain how Paul, who in the same letter argues so strongly that salvation is by faith, suddenly says that people are automatically saved by the work of Christ. Besides, the first statement in this couplet does not refer to every human being. Christ has to be left out of this statement. He was not condemned by virtue of Adam's sin, because he was without sin. So even there "all" is not absolute.

The context shows that Paul is talking about two races of humans. The first is Adam's race. It includes all those who sin and thus are under condemnation. The second is Christ's race. They are the people who are "in Christ"—that is, those who through faith have received salvation. Verse 17 says almost the same thing as verse 18, but it confines those belonging to the second group to "those who receive God's abundant provision of grace"—"For if, by the trespass of the one man, death reigned through that one man, how much more will those who receive God's abundant provision . . . reign in life through the one man, Jesus Christ."

So the context demands that "all" in the second part of Romans 5:18 must be confined to those who are "in Christ." These are the people who, as Paul taught in the first five chapters of Romans, have been justified by faith. He is saying that just as the whole human race was led into condemnation through the sin of Adam, the whole new race of those in Christ is led into salvation through the righteous act of Christ.

The next passage with a parallel couplet is 1 Corinthians 15:22, which gives a message quite similar to Romans 5:18. It says, "For as in Adam all die, so in Christ all will be made alive." Here too if the parallelism were carried out absolutely, we would have to conclude that every human being will experience a blessed resurrection at the end. But here too the context shows that such an interpretation is impossible.

Often in this chapter Paul says that the great cost of Christian discipleship is worthwhile because those in Christ, unlike unbelievers, will experience the resurrection (see vv. 19, 31, 32; see also v.

58). Four times in the verses surrounding verse 22 Paul says that it is those who are in Christ or who belong to Christ who are raised (vv. 18, 19, 20, 23). Surely then, we must conclude that when he says, ". . . in Christ all will be made alive" he means that it is those who belong to Christ's race—that is, those "in Christ"—who will be resurrected.

So the second "all" in these two texts refers to all those who are in Christ, and that includes only those who believe.

UNIVERSALISTIC THEOLOGIES

Out of the biblical insistence on the universality of Christ's work have arisen various universalistic theologies.

Karl Barth

The first of these is associated with the Swiss theologian Karl Barth (1886-1968). Barth placed a great emphasis on man's utter sinfulness and his inability to save himself. He also placed a great emphasis on the total sufficiency of the work of Christ for our salvation. These two emphases came as a breath of fresh air into a theological arena dominated by liberalism's emphasis on human effort. Barth's approach to Christ's work has been described as objective as opposed to the subjective approaches of liberalism.

Barth, however, carried his objectivism to an extreme. In stressing that Christ has done everything that is necessary for our justification, he also seemed to say that man does not have to do anything in order to receive it. In a study of Romans 5 he said, "In sovereign anticipation of our faith God has justified [people] through the sacrificial blood of Christ."[4] He explained this idea further by saying, "In his own death [Jesus Christ] makes their peace with God—*before* they themselves have decided for that peace and *quite apart from that decision*."[5] It is evident from these quotes that

Barth does not think that the act of believing is as critical as biblical theology usually holds.

Barth places so much emphasis on the fact that Christ bore the punishment for our sins that he can't see people as being under God's wrath anymore. So he says that godless people are grasping back to an objective impossibility. They are attempting to expose themselves again "to the threat which has already been executed and consequently removed."[6] He says that "for all their godlessness they are unable to restore the perversity for whose removal [Christ] surrendered himself and so rekindle the fire of divine wrath which he has borne."[7]

It is clear that the logical conclusion of this type of thinking is universalism. Barth knew this, but he himself refused to take the step that leads to universalism. Many others, however, took that step, and it is acknowledged that Barth's theology provided a big impetus to the movement towards universalism within the church.[8]

Those who take the step which Barth refused to take view salvation and evangelism in the way described in the Evangelism Sunday sermon I heard: evangelism is telling people that they have been saved and that they can now experience the benefits of salvation.

Friedrich Schleiermacher

The German theologian Friedrich Schleiermacher (1768-1834) held a doctrine of absolute predestination. However, he rejected the double predestination of the Calvinists, which restricted election only to a certain group of people. He regarded this as arbitrary and incompatible with the biblical picture of God. He said, "It shatters the sense of racial unity generated in us by God's grace."[9] So he emerged with the view that every human being has been predestined to salvation and will finally be saved. Using words similar to those of Barth, he said, "God regards all men only in Christ."[10]

We will make only two brief points in response to these universalistic theologies. The first is that they do not do justice to the biblical insistence upon faith in Christ as a condition for salvation. In fact, it is the two so-called universalistic bodies of Scripture, the writings of John and Paul, that talk most about faith. The verb "to believe" (*pisteuo*) appears ninety-eight times in the Gospel of John. It is Paul who gives the most comprehensive treatment of justification by faith in the Bible. This means that the biblical writers who emphasized the universality of Christ's work most are the ones who emphasized the need for faith in Christ most.

John 3:18 says, "Whoever believes in him is not condemned, but whoever does not believe stands condemned already because he has not believed in the name of God's one and only Son." John 8:24 says, "If you do not believe that I am the one I claim to be, you will indeed die in your sins." In the first four chapters of the Epistle to the Romans, Paul argues for the necessity of faith for justification. This is not the faith which Christ exercised, as some claim. It is the faith which we exercise. Romans 4:5 asserts: "To the man who does not work but trusts God who justifies the wicked, *his* faith is credited as righteousness."

Michael Griffiths has explained the relation between the work of Christ and the response of faith in this way: "The cross is sufficient for all, but efficient only for those who will . . . make the necessary response of repentance and faith. . . . The cross without faith is like a vaccine without a syringe."[11]

Our second point is that while the Bible states that Jesus bore God's wrath for our sin, as Barth rightly insisted, it also says that those who do not believe in Christ are still under wrath. They will have, in the end, to face this wrath at the judgment. Romans 2:5-9 describes this. Paul addresses the sinner and says, "Because of your stubbornness and your unrepentant heart, you are storing up wrath against yourself for the day of God's wrath, when his righteous judgment will be revealed" (v. 5). On that day of judgment "there will be wrath and anger" and "trouble and distress" for those who reject the truth (vv. 8, 9; see also 2 Thess. 1:7-9).

The conclusion we draw is that while Christ is potentially the Savior of all, he is actually the Savior only of those who respond to his salvation in faith.

CHAPTER SIX

WILL CHRIST'S FINAL VICTORY BE INCOMPLETE?

H.S. Reimarus, one of the pioneers of nineteenth-century German skeptical criticism of the New Testament, said that he could not accept a religion which presents a way of salvation and still implies that only about one-tenth of those that lived would go to heaven. William Temple, the famous Archbishop of Canterbury, wrote, "How can there be a paradise for any while there is a hell for some?" He continues that there could not be a paradise for a mother if her child were in hell.[1]

In this chapter we will see whether the traditional view of the last days implies that God's final victory will be incomplete.

ONLY A FEW SAVED IN THE END?

Does the Bible teach that only one-tenth of those who lived will be saved, as Reimarus claims? There is a whole body of Scripture that describes a great turning to God at the last day. I believe that this anticipated turning to God will more than "even things out" in the end.[2]

A great ingathering is implied in the following promises God made to Abraham: ". . . all peoples on earth will be blessed"; "I will make your offspring like the dust of the earth, so that if anyone could count the dust, then your offspring could be counted" (Gen. 12:3; 13:16; see also 15:5; 26:4, 5). Today we regard Abraham's offspring as the spiritual Israel—those who through faith have been reckoned as righteous.

The Psalms look forward to the reign of the Messiah extending to the far corners of the earth. Psalm 22:27, 28 says, "All the ends of the earth will remember and turn to the Lord, and all the families of the nations will bow down before him, for dominion belongs to the Lord and he rules over the nations." Psalm 72, which became the basis for Isaac Watts's famous hymn "Jesus Shall Reign," says, "In his days the righteous will flourish; prosperity will abound till the moon is no more. He will rule from sea to sea and from the River to the ends of the earth" (vv. 7, 8). The promise to Abraham is echoed in verse 17: "All nations will be blessed through him, and they will call him blessed." The Psalm concludes with the hope that "the whole earth [will] be filled with his glory" (v. 19).

Isaiah 11:9, 10 says that in the messianic age "the earth will be full of the knowledge of the Lord as the waters cover the sea" and looks forward to the day when "the Root of Jesse will stand as a banner for the peoples; the nations will rally to him, and his place of rest will be glorious" (see also Hab. 2:14).

Today we see the stage being set for this great day as the gospel goes out into all the world and takes root in the different cultures of the world. Christ predicted this when he described the growth of the Kingdom of God through the parables of the mustard seed and the leaven (Matt. 13:31-33). David Barrett says, in the *World Christian Encyclopedia*, that "in Jesus' day the rapid growth of a mustard seed startled his followers; in the same way today, the vast expansion of the influence of the kingdom of God exceeds all the expectations of the earlier generations of Christians."[3] Church historian Kenneth Scott Latourette said in 1948, "Christianity, so history leads us confidently to predict, is in its youth and is to continue to mount as a factor in the human scene."[4]

Jesus placed premium value on the preaching of the gospel as a factor that determines the time of the climax of human history. He said, "This gospel of the kingdom will be preached in the whole world as a testimony to all nations, and then the end will come" (Matt. 24:14).

Paul refers to this great turning to God in Romans 11. He says that after "the full number of the Gentiles has come in . . . all Israel will be saved" (vv. 25, 26). Later he says that "God has bound all men over to disobedience so that he may have mercy on them all" (v. 32).

Now these verses don't teach that every Jew and every human that ever lived will be saved, as C. H. Dodd and Ethelbert Stauffer claim. In Romans 9—11 Paul was dealing with the problem of Israel's rejection of their promised Messiah. He earlier described how this came about. Now he says that this rejection is not a permanent one. The day will come when the nation of Israel will turn to Christ, though that does not mean that each and every person in the nation will be saved.[5]

The book of Revelation also looks forward to such a day, claiming that in heaven there will be "a great multitude that no one could count, from every nation, tribe, people and language, standing before the throne and in front of the Lamb." These are redeemed people, for, John says, "they were wearing white robes and were holding palm branches in their hands" (Rev. 7:9).

Though we cannot be sure when and how this final ingathering will take place, Revelation gives us some hints about it, saying that Satan will be "bound . . . for a thousand years . . . to keep him from deceiving the nations" (Rev. 20:2, 3). We know that in this age Satan "has blinded the minds of unbelievers, so that they cannot see the light of the gospel of the glory of Christ" (2 Cor. 4:4). If he is bound and kept from deceiving people for an extended period of time, then we can expect this period to be a time of great turning to God. This could be the time described in 1 Corinthians 15:25 when Christ reigns "until he has put all his enemies under his feet." After this, Christ is going to hand over the Kingdom to God (v. 24). The enemies spoken of here could be those demonic forces whose influence keeps people from following God.

The Scriptures, however, do not teach that every single person who ever lived will be saved. Yet I believe that the final turning to God will more than even things out in terms of the effectiveness of God's plan to save the world. With the population of the world multiplying at such a rapid rate, we can expect the population at the end of time to represent a significant portion of the entire number of humans that ever lived on earth.

Alongside the body of Scripture we have presented above we must place those texts which predict that in the last days evil is going to have a final reign of terror on earth. Different approaches have been adopted to harmonize these two bodies of Scripture. But that subject is not within the scope of this book.

CAN THE BLISS OF HEAVEN COEXIST WITH HELL?

We now come to William Temple's argument that a mother could not know bliss in heaven if her child were in hell. Nels Ferre says, "If hell were eternal . . . heaven would be an eternal place of mourning. All those in truly agape fellowship would identify their lot with the lost." He says, "Heaven can be heaven only when it has emptied hell."[6]

Even though Ferre thinks that the bliss of heaven cannot coexist with the misery of hell, the Bible teaches that it can. Revelation 21 has a comprehensive description of the bliss of heaven. It contains the famous statement that God "will wipe every tear from their eyes. There will be no more death or mourning or crying or pain" (v. 4). But this passage also says that "the cowardly, the unbelieving, the vile . . . —their place will be in the fiery lake of burning sulfur. This is the second death" (v. 8; see also v. 27).

But how can heaven and hell coexist without the latter spoiling the experience of the former? We must remember that God is often praised for the justness of his judgments in the book of Revelation:

> Then I heard the angel in charge of the waters say: "You are just in these judgments, you who are and were, the Holy One, because you have so judged; for they have shed the blood of your saints and prophets, and you have given them blood to drink as they deserve." And I heard the altar respond: "Yes, Lord God Almighty, true and just are your judgments." (Rev. 16:5-7; see also 6:10; 18:20; 19:1-3)

Now the praise is given to God for the punishment of murderers of the faithful. From this exceptional case we may derive a principle that is universally true: when we realize that God's judgments are just, we will praise him. It would be wrong to say that we will rejoice with the type of selfish glee that those on earth have when they see their enemies abased. Rather, people will accept the justness of judgment.

With this background we come to the problem of loved ones in hell. It would seem that the love which causes us to mourn over their loss and the holiness which causes us to praise God for his judgments are opposed to each other. Here we come to the age-old problem of harmonizing love with holiness; this will be discussed in Chapter 10. Yet even on earth we sometimes see this harmony. When a parent agrees with the decision of his son's employer to dismiss the son for doing something wrong, he exhibits this harmony of love and holiness. We see this very rarely on earth because usually our love is warped by unholiness. That is why leaders are generally advised to stay clear of controversies involving their family members. They cannot be objective because of emotional family ties.

In heaven we will be freed from the subjectivity brought about by emotional ties. So we will be able to agree *wholeheartedly* with the judgment of God upon our lost loved ones. This will remove much of the pain of what we see. Perhaps there will be regret over the loss of the person. But, as we will show below, there will not be the type of sorrow which takes out the brightness of life. If this is so, there will be no tears and no night in heaven.

Can perfect joy exist when there is regret? I believe it can. Even today we see something of this. When a loved one lives in sin, we are sorry but not bitter. This is because no human relationship is absolutely basic to our existence. Only our relationship with God is absolutely basic. This is why Jesus said that we must, if necessary, be willing to jeopardize our relationship with our own family members for his sake (Matt. 10:34-37). A Christian can know the complete fulfillment which Christ gives even though a very close loved one opposes the way of Christ. This type of "joy in the Lord" is alien to the thinking of most people, because the contemporary idea of joy is a temporal and shallow one based on circumstances.

The fact that human ties are not basic to life is accentuated in heaven. Christ himself said that "at the resurrection people will neither marry nor be given in marriage; they will be like the angels in heaven" (Matt. 22:30). Paul said that the marriage bond of a woman is broken once her husband dies (Rom. 7:1-3).

On earth, because we are limited by mortality, we cannot love everyone equally. Only God has a capacity for a love big enough to do that. So on earth we express active and intense love to people with whom we have special ties, such as our family members and those we are called to serve. It is not humanly possible for us to be responsible for people we have never seen. Heaven is a place where love is perfected. Everyone is free to love everyone else in the way that Christ loves them. In such a place the ties that were significant on earth lose their special significance.

There will be a diminishing of the special value of earthly ties in heaven, and hence the reality of earthly loved ones being in hell will be something bearable. In heaven we will be enraptured by the glory of Christ. Thus we will need no human ties for our fulfillment. While there will be regret about the loss of loved ones, our thoughts will be so fully in harmony with the holiness of God that we will agree wholeheartedly about the judgment that is given to them. And because we have "come to terms" with the judgment, we are not hindered from experiencing fullness of joy.

WILL HEAVEN BE INCOMPLETE?

But if some people for whom Christ died are in hell, will not heaven be incomplete and hence less than glorious? There is indeed a sense in which heaven will be incomplete. But that will not make it inglorious. The fact that many unworthy sinners were given such a wonderful gift as a place in heaven will in itself be a cause for immense glory in heaven. The greatest surprise is not that some are lost, but that any people should be saved at all.

Those in hell lose their status as precious humans following the judgment. So their absence will not cause a void in heaven. While the door of opportunity was open, they were potential citizens of heaven and they received the blessings of God's common or prevenient grace that was available to all humanity. Now that day of opportunity is over, and they have forfeited their chance to be part of the new humanity. Those who are saved form the new humanity, and they will be in heaven in full strength.

EVERY KNEE SHALL BOW

The universalist would not be satisfied yet. He would point to texts that describe Christ's victory in a way that suggests that all will be saved. Ethelbert Stauffer claims that Paul's later epistles teach this "universal homecoming."[7]

Philippians 2:10, 11 is a favorite universalist text: ". . . at the name of Jesus every knee should bow, in heaven and on earth and under the earth, and every tongue confess that Jesus Christ is Lord, to the glory of God the Father." Usually when we say that a person bows his or her knee at the name of Jesus or confesses that Jesus Christ is Lord, we mean that this person is one who has received salvation. If this is the case here, then this text teaches universalism. But it is not so.

This text is a quotation from Isaiah 45:23. Paul quoted this verse in Romans 14:11 in a way that eliminates a universalistic interpretation. There Paul says, "We will all stand before God's judgment seat" (14:10). Then he quotes from Isaiah: "It is written: 'As surely as I live,' says the Lord, 'every knee will bow before me; every tongue will confess to God.'" Then, as if to further explain what he is saying, Paul says, "So then, each of us will give an account of himself to God" (14:12). Paul is describing the judgment. He uses Isaiah 45:23 to say that every one is accountable to God and will have to pay their homage to him at the judgment. He is not talking about salvation. F. F. Bruce paraphrases Romans 14:11b as, "Every tongue shall make humble acknowledgement to God."[8]

We argue that Paul uses Isaiah 45:23 to refer to acknowledgment rather than salvation in the Philippians passage too. Philippians 2:9-11 describes the exaltation of the once-humiliated Lord—not salvation. Though Jesus humbled himself and temporarily gave victory to the forces of evil, in the end of time all will humbly acknowledge that he is Lord. Paul believed that Jesus is going to reign until he puts all his enemies under him (1 Cor. 15:24-28; see also Phil. 3:21). What Paul describes in Philippians is the culmination of that process.

Such acknowledgment is not the same as salvation. Evil spirits acknowledged that Jesus is "the Holy One of God" (Mark 1:24); but they were not saved. In the parable about Lazarus, the rich man acknowledged the truth and even asked that Lazarus be sent to earth to preach it to his relatives; but he was not saved (Luke 16:27-31). The demons believe there is one God; rather than giving them salvation, it makes them shudder (Jas. 2:19). For salvation one must not only confess with the mouth that Jesus is Lord but also *believe in the heart* (Rom. 10:9). Philippians 2:11 must include the joyous acknowledgment of Christ's Lordship by the saved, for every knee and tongue is included in it. But for the lost, who have been defeated by Christ, this will be an acknowledgment of fear and regret.

ALL IN ALL

1 Corinthians 15:28 is perhaps the favorite universalist text. It has been cited by William Barclay, C. H. Dodd, Nels Ferre, Ethelbert Stauffer, John A. T. Robinson and others in support of universalism. It states that in the end, "God [will] be all in all."

What does this statement mean? In verse 24a Paul says, "Then the end will come, when [Christ] hands over the kingdom to God the Father." But this will happen only "after he has destroyed all dominion, authority and power" (v. 24b). Verses 25-27 describe what this process of destruction of enemies will be like. Verse 28b describes the situation after Christ hands over the Kingdom to God: God will be "all in all." It does not address the issue of who will enter the Kingdom. What it says is that after the Kingdom is handed over to God, God will be "all in all."

Earlier on in the book of Corinthians (6:9-11) Paul gave his ideas about who will enter the Kingdom. He said that "the wicked will not enter the kingdom of God" (v. 9a). He then amplified this by listing some examples of wicked people (vv. 9b, 10). Then he contrasted them with his readers, who also once belonged to the category of the wicked, but have now been "washed," "sanctified" and "justified" (v. 11). They will enter the Kingdom. First Corinthians 6:9-11, therefore, tells us who will and who will not enter the Kingdom. First Corinthians 15:28 tells us what life in the Kingdom will be like.

In the very next paragraph (vv. 29-34) Paul writes as one who believes that some will be lost in the end. So the context of this passage also makes a universalistic interpretation highly unlikely.

From the above reasoning, we conclude that the situation of God being "all in all" should be confined to the future Kingdom and that this Kingdom does not include all of humanity.

ALL THINGS RECONCILED

Colossians 1:19, 20 says, "For God was pleased to have all his fullness dwell in him, and through him to reconcile to himself all things, whether things on earth or things in heaven, by making peace through his blood, shed on the cross." C. H. Dodd and Ethelbert Stauffer claim that when Paul said "all things" and added "whether things on earth or things in heaven" he must have included in that description all human beings. While some scholars would dispute this, we agree that all humanity should be included here. However, we do not agree that the *salvation* of all people is intended. We believe that what is intended is a reconciliation of all creation whereby its rebellion is crushed and it is made to conform to the plan of God.

In verse 20 Paul was talking about the whole creation, but in verses 21-23 he switches to the realm of personal reconciliation. He says, "Once you were alienated from God . . . but now he has reconciled you" (vv. 21, 22a). The end of this work of reconciliation is final salvation: "He has reconciled you . . . to present you holy in his sight, without blemish and free from accusation" (v. 22). Not everyone will receive this final salvation. Paul goes on to say that they will receive this only "if you continue in your faith, established and firm, not moved from the hope held out in the gospel" (v. 23). So while cosmic reconciliation is universal and unrestricted (v. 20), personal reconciliation is restricted to those who are faithful (v. 23). A similar restriction is implied in verses 26-28.

Colossians 2:15 also implies that there is a difference between cosmic and personal reconciliation. Here Paul describes how the work of Christ affected the evil powers: "And having disarmed the powers and authorities, he made a public spectacle of them, triumphing over them by the cross." This is a work of destruction rather than of salvation, and it is a result of the work of Christ on the cross. So the same reconciling work of Christ which causes the salvation of some individuals also causes the destruction of the forces of evil. If we are to take the reconciliation of all things as meaning the salvation of all things, then we will have to hold that Paul is including the salvation of fallen angels in 1:20. F. F. Bruce points out that this goes against the whole trend of the Bible's, and especially Paul's, teaching about the destiny of these enemies of God.[9]

It is best, therefore, to distinguish between cosmic and personal reconciliation. Paul did this in 2 Corinthians 5:19, 20. He said, "God was reconciling the world to himself in Christ" (v. 19a). Then he went on to say that "he has committed to us the message of reconciliation" so that "we implore [others] on Christ's behalf: Be reconciled to God" (vv. 19b, 20). Only those who actively accept Christ's work of cosmic reconciliation will in fact be personally reconciled to God.

Bruce explains the reconciliation mentioned in Colossians 1:20 thus: "The peace effected by the death of Christ may be freely accepted, or it may be imposed willy-nilly. The reconciliation of the universe includes what would otherwise be distinguished as pacification." Bruce says, "By his reconciling work 'The host of the high ones on high' [Isa. 24:21] and sinful human beings on earth have been decisively subdued to the will of God and ultimately they can but subserve his purpose, whether they please or not."[10] So universal salvation is not intended by this verse.

COSMIC SALVATION

I will briefly mention a trend which is gaining prominence in Christian circles that can be described by the term "cosmic salvation." Its roots are varied. But its popularity could be attributed, at least in part, to the return to prominence of pantheistic thinking.

Pantheism claims that everything that exists is divine. It is related to monism, which holds that there is only one reality, the divine. Pantheism is one of the foundational aspects of Hindu thinking and is now seen in the New Age movements of the West.

The area of interest for us is the pantheistic idea of the indissoluble link between God and man. Philosophically that makes it impossible for people to be lost and eternally separated from God, for man is of the same essence as God. The goal in pantheistic thinking is to see everything that there is as being absorbed into the Absolute or the Divine. So this view is a major alternative to the Christian view of salvation and damnation, and it could become a more prominent factor in the future.

Recently we have seen some formulations within the "Christian" orbit which show affinities to the pantheistic scheme. These have sometimes been called the "cosmic christologies," where the salvation wrought by Christ is said to be of cosmic proportions to the extent that everything created is brought into union with Christ.

An influential Hindu leader, Keshub Chandra Sen (1838-1884), spoke of Christ's pantheism and believed that India will reach Christ through the Vedantic Hindu creed of absorption and immersion in the divine.[11] He saw the pre-existent Logos as the beginning of creation, and its perfection. He said that "the culmination of humanity is the Divine Son." He asked, "Is the process of evolution really over? If sonship there was, it was bound to develop itself not in one solitary individual but in all humanity." He went on to say, "Surely universal salvation is the purpose of creation."[12] He saw this as the state when everyone becomes Christ.

More recently, the French Jesuit priest and paleontologist Pierre Teilhard de Chardin (1881-1955) presented a similar view. He was greatly influenced by the idea of an ever-evolving universe. He saw such evolution moving toward what he called the "Omega point." This took place by an evolutionary process that he called "Centerism"—the tendency of all things to converge, to move toward the center. The eventual outcome of this process will be a complete unity in the universe. In this unity everything will be part of a completed organic whole. Even the religions will be united.

All that de Chardin proposes will happen is to be accomplished by the cosmic Christ. He describes his Omega point as a "Christosphere" where God is all in all. He describes this scheme as a "very real pantheism." When asked about hell, he said that if the Church says there is a hell, he will agree. But he looked beyond hell to the Omega point.[13]

I do not consider myself sufficiently acquainted with the thought of Sen and de Chardin to adequately critique them. I would only say that their grand schemes have no basis in the Scriptures. The only way that we could connect them with the Scriptures is by introducing a philosophical system which is alien to the thinking of the scriptural writers and imposing it upon the text. Thus it is made to say something very different from what the authors intended it to say.

CHAPTER SEVEN

WHAT ABOUT REINCARNATION?

It is estimated that about 50 percent of the world's population believes in reincarnation. It is the predominant view in Asia. A 1982 Gallup poll revealed that in the United States of America about 23 percent of the population held some form of it.[1] In Europe the figure was 21 percent in 1986.[2]

Reincarnation is gaining ground in Christian circles too. The Gallup poll mentioned above found that 17 percent of those who said they regularly attend church believed it. Albert Schweitzer is reported to have said that it was "a most comforting explanation of reality." Quincy Howe, Jr., in his book *Reincarnation for the Christian*, says, "One of the most attractive aspects of reincarnation is that it removes entirely the possibility of damnation."[3] Howe and other influential writers like British philosopher John Hick and American Anglican philosopher Geddes MacGregor are presenting reincarnation as a fitting alternative to what they regard as the "horrible" (Hick) and "abhorrent" (Howe) idea of everlasting punishment.

VARIETIES OF THE BELIEF

Greek philosophers like Plato and Pythagoras believed in reincarnation, but its present expressions are more influenced by Hindu philosophy. Hindus believe in the "transmigration of the soul." Through the operation of the law of *karma*, which keeps track of one's life, an individual's soul is said to be incarnated in another body which is born immediately or some time after his death.

The process goes on for thousands, possibly millions, of incarnations. Moral lessons are learned during this evolution of the soul. When sufficient merit has been earned to warrant liberation from the cycle of rebirths, the soul achieves salvation or *moksha* and becomes fully absorbed into the Absolute or Divine.

Orthodox Buddhists use the term rebirth rather than reincarnation because of the Buddhist doctrine of no-soul or *anatta*. Instead of a soul being transmigrated, here it is a bundle of characteristics or attributes representing the net effect of the outworking of the law of *karma* which gathers energy to give rise to a new individual. The goal in Buddhism is to escape from the present existence, which entails suffering, and attain *Nirvana*.

Despite recent attempts to present the Buddhist and Hindu views in a positive light, they remain dreary because of the long time taken to achieve liberation. The Hindu view of history, which is cyclic and does not see history moving to any sort of climax, is thus devoid of hope.

The western forms of the belief which are found in the flourishing New Age movements have a much brighter outlook. Analysts have linked these positive, hope-filled aspects to the fact that the New Age movements have grown in cultures influenced by Christianity, where hope plays an important part. They teach a hope for new and better lives in the future without the dreary cycle stretching over millions of years.

THE BIBLE AND REINCARNATION

"Christian" reincarnationists try to find the doctrine in the Bible. But now there are few who take that claim seriously. I will briefly mention the four texts most commonly used by reincarnationists.

In John 3:3 Jesus says, "I tell you the truth, no one can see the kingdom of God unless he is born again." Nicodemus responds with a note of sarcasm: "How can a man be born when he is old? . . . Surely he cannot enter a second time into his mother's womb to be born!" (3:4). Nicodemus thinks the idea of reincarnation is impossible. Jesus confirms this and explains that he is talking of a spiritual rebirth: "I tell you the truth, unless a man is born of water and the Spirit, he cannot enter the kingdom of God" (3:5). He then explains what he means by spiritual rebirth. Certainly reincarnation is not meant here.

References to John the Baptist being a supposed reincarnation of Elijah are more popular. Jesus said of John, "If you are willing to accept it, he is the Elijah who was to come" (Matt. 11:14). Reincarnationists say Jesus believed John was an incarnation of Elijah. Quincy Howe has built a case for this in a most ingenious way. He says there seems to be evidence that the first-century community known as the Essenes believed in reincarnation. This is presented by a route of argumentation that is by no means convincing. Then he says that John the Baptist was probably influenced by the Essenes. And then he says that Jesus was probably influenced by John.[4] Howe also says that for the prophecy of Malachi 4:5 "to be fully realized, John the Baptist must *be* Elijah."[5] This prophecy says, "See, I will send you the prophet Elijah before that great and dreadful day of the Lord comes."

Without responding to Howe's scheme here I will show that the tie between Elijah and John the Baptist related to the nature of their ministries rather than the identity of their persons. This is what Zacharias said about him: "And he will go on before the Lord, in the spirit and power of Elijah" (Luke 1:17). What this means is well illustrated in the final conversation between Elijah and his successor, Elisha. Elijah asks Elisha, "What can I do for you before I am taken from you?" Elisha says, "Let me inherit a double portion of your spirit" (2 Kgs. 2:9). After Elijah had been taken up to heaven, "The company of the prophets from Jericho, who were watching, said, 'The spirit of Elijah is resting on Elisha'" (v. 15). Elisha was going to continue the type of ministry that Elijah had. This is what John did also.

John specifically said that he was not Elijah (John 1:21). Yet Jesus saw John's ministry as the fulfillment of Malachi's prophecy. He said, "He is the Elijah who was to come" (Matt. 11:14; see also 17:12, 13).

Besides, Elijah never died. He was taken up to heaven, like Enoch. And Enoch "did not experience death" (Heb. 11:5). It must have been the same for Elijah. When he appeared on the Mount of Transfiguration, he appeared not as John but as Elijah.

This is an example of biblical typology. John fulfilled the role of Elijah as prophesied by Malachi. And as in all type-antitype comparisons, the type (John) was superior to the antitype (Elijah). Jesus says he was "more than a prophet" (Matt. 11:9).

In John 9:1-3 the disciples ask Jesus regarding a man born blind, "Who sinned, this man or his parents, that he was born blind?" MacGregor and Howe use this to show that the Bible accepts reincarnation. F. F. Bruce says that this question may have been influenced by the teachings of some rabbis that an infant might sin while in the womb. Bruce thinks "it is less likely that they thought he might have sinned in a previous existence."[6]

If the disciples did indeed consider the prenatal sin explanation as a possible option, Jesus corrects them in his response to their question: "Neither this man nor his parents sinned, but this happened so that the work of God might be displayed in his life" (v. 3). His answer also denies the reincarnation option, which says that the present fortunes of people are influenced by their former lives.

The other passages cited by "Christian" reincarnationists

such as 1 Corinthians 15, Hebrews 7:3, and James 3:6 can also upon careful study be discounted as giving support to that view.

PAST-LIFE RECALL

Sri Lankan newspapers often carry articles about people who recall their past lives. Many believe these cases provide conclusive evidence for reincarnation. There are two types of past-life recall. The first is "hypnotic regression" where subjects are led, through hypnosis, to delve into their past lives. The second, which happens most often with children, is "spontaneous recall." Here the subject, without the help of an intermediary, claims to have been someone else and talks of his past life.

Many of the cases of recall lend themselves to natural explanations. In hypnotic regression there is inducement from an outside influence, which causes one to raise questions about the dependability of this method. The subject is asked to remember previous lives, which means that he is expected to believe that he did indeed have past lives. Mark Albrecht tells of a case where a hypnotist progressed—rather than regressed—an actor, Robert Cummins, into his future. He said that he was going to be born in 1989 in Canton, China, where he would become a doctor. Albrecht comments that "the entire episode as described is identical to hypnotic regressions of past lives in both details and results, raising yet more vexing questions about the nature of hypnosis."[7]

Then there is the amazing capacity of our subconscious minds to store data. Someone has said that we use only about 10 percent of what is in our brains. Much of what we read and hear is said to be stored in our molecular "memory bank." This phenomenon is called cryptoamnesia. These details can emerge under special conditions. One person under hypnosis spoke Oscan, a third-century B.C. Italian language. Later it was discovered that he had looked at an Oscan grammar in a library a few days before the hypnosis experience. Several phrases had registered in his subconscious mind and found expression in the hypnotic stage.[8]

We must also bear in mind the possibility of cultural and religious conditioning. In most cases of past-life recall the subjects were "surrounded by a cultural and religious milieu that encouraged belief in reincarnation."[9] Most cases of spontaneous recall are children. All this reduces the credibility of many of these "evidences" for reincarnation.

Yet there may be a few cases left that cannot be explained naturally. Could these not be spiritistic or demonic phenomena? We must remember, as Albrecht points out, that "a great majority of cases [of past-life recall] exhibit features parallel with those of spiritism, seances, mediumship and demonic possession."[10] The Bible teaches that demons and spirits can possess people and, in various other ways, do great harm. "Satan himself masquerades as an angel of light" (2 Cor. 11:14). He does this with a view to deceiving people.

Could it not be that some of the cases of past-life recall are supernatural actions of Satan and his forces, intended to deceive people and further confirm them in their unbelief? After all, one of Satan's functions is to blind "the minds of unbelievers, so that they cannot see the light of the gospel of the glory of Christ" (2 Cor. 4:4). If the gospel is the truth and therefore reincarnation is untrue, then, by giving supposed evidence for reincarnation, Satan would be achieving his objective of deceiving people and confirming them in their unbelief.

IS ONE LIFE SPAN INSUFFICIENT?

Reincarnationists argue for the superiority of their position on the grounds that one life span is not enough to perfect a person. Sylvia Cranston says that "it seems an inexcusable waste of resources" to restrict human beings to "but one sojourn on earth" because the earth "affords almost illimitable opportunities for growth of intelligence, talents and moral powers."[11]

But is there evidence that people are progressing in terms of the quality of their life? There is no evidence that people are getting better with each life when one looks at the world. Actually things may be getting worse. People have vastly increased their knowledge, but that has not made them better people.

The world is *not* getting better, because of the fallen nature of humanity. Indeed, if salvation was to be earned by our own merits, one life would not suffice. But because of our fallen nature, even a thousand lives would not suffice. We need a Savior. We need God's grace to help us out of our predicament. This argument for reincarnation cannot stand because it does not adequately address the problem of man's fallen nature.

Most reincarnationists admit that the goal of perfection will take an unimaginably long time to achieve. Buddhists agree that very few people, if any, have attained *Nirvana* since Buddha. If, as Buddhism expounds, all existence on earth entails suffering, and if freedom from this suffering is thousands of lives away, we are left with a very gloomy prospect.

Yet many people prefer this scheme to that of receiving salvation on the merits of Christ's work. In order to receive Christ's salvation one must first admit that he cannot save himself. People would rather work at a difficult scheme, which gives them the satisfaction of earning their salvation, than admit that they cannot help themselves. The scheme of reincarnation based on one's own *karma* gives them this satisfaction. So, despite its bleak prospects of success, people would rather have this scheme than admit their helplessness and their need for grace.

The gospel is good news to one who admits that it is fruitless to try to earn his salvation. My grandmother was orphaned when she was still a teenager. Her husband died when she was in her thirties. It seemed that she was suffering for the bad *karma* she had accrued through previous births. She did everything her religion, Buddhism, could offer to offset this *karma*. But nothing seemed to work. In her hopeless state she considered the Christian gospel. She discovered the good news that Christ had already paid for her bad *karma*, and she did not need to suffer for it anymore. She became a Christian! Her life was such a powerful witness that we consider her the spiritual matriarch of a whole "clan" of descendants who are servants of Christ.

GLORIFICATION: TOO SUDDEN A CHANGE?

Reincarnationists object that the scheme of perfection through glorification after death is too sudden to be realistic. Geddes MacGregor says, "On the reincarnationist view, one little life of whatever length . . . is not enough to weed out the garden of the soul. . . . The purificatory process takes a far longer time than we are likely to imagine."[12] They claim that reincarnation gives a more realistic answer to the question of the destiny of the human soul.

Norman Geisler and Yutuka Amano respond that "the gap between a perfect God and imperfect human beings is so great, there will always be an infinite difference between the goodness of God and the goodness of man."[13] A thousand lives would not suffice to bring us to a point anywhere near perfection. We need God's grace. It is when we lose sight of grace that we come to positions advocating human striving after salvation.

John Hick thinks that the radical change that takes place at glorification is unrealistic. So drastic is this change that after death a different person is said to be in heaven.[14] We disagree! The most radical change to take place in a person's life occurs at conversion.[15] That changes his life-orientation. After that his citizenship is in heaven, and his heart is set on heavenly things. Glorification consummates those already existing desires and experiences. So the change at conversion is more radical than the transformation at glorification.

THE INJUSTICE OF REINCARNATION

In the reincarnation scheme, a completely new person is born. This person is influenced by the *karma* of a person who lived before him and about whom he knows nothing.

R. C. Sproul has pointed out that "memory is a vital element of personal identity." A person may not remember everything he did, but he is aware of his past. He has a personal history of which he is conscious. Sproul says, "If I lived before in the past, I have no memory of it whatsoever. That spells radical *discontinuity* of personal existence." His conclusion is that "to live again with no recollection of the past is no different an experience than to have died once forever."[16] In that sense it is wrong to use the words *reincarnation* and *rebirth*, as it is a completely new individual who is born.

This brings us to the question of the fairness of this scheme. Is it fair that someone should suffer for things done by a complete stranger? Hitler, for example, would not have to pay for his sins. When the going gets tough, he simply commits suicide. Somebody who is born after him has to pay for the things that he did. And this poor person does not know that he is paying for Hitler's sins. In fact he may personally find Hitler's atrocities repulsive to contemplate!

John Hick attempts to solve this problem with his ingenious suggestion that the person is reincarnated in another world with full recollection of what he was in his earlier life. But this is pure speculation.

The doctrine of judgment is more fair than this. And the Christian message that the spotless Son of God willingly suffered to pull us out of our sad lot, for which we are personally responsible, is good news to all.

CHAPTER EIGHT

GOD'S WILL TO SAVE ALL

The logic of the situation is simple. Either God could not or would not save all. If he could not, he is not sovereign, then not all things are possible with God. If he would not, again the New Testament is wrong, for it openly claims that God would have all to be saved.[1]

These words of Nels Ferre present one of the most popular arguments against an eternal hell. If God desires all to be saved and all things are possible with him, then all should be saved.[2]

THE BIBLICAL TEXTS

Two texts specifically proclaim God's desire to save all. The first is 1 Timothy 2:3, 4. Paul had just urged that Christians make "prayers . . . for *everyone*" (v. 1). Then he says that by "everyone" he means "kings and *all* those in authority. . . ." Then comes our text: "This is good and pleases God our Savior, who wants *all* men to be saved and to come to a knowledge of the truth." Then Paul presents

Christ as the Mediator between God and men (v. 5) and the one "who gave himself as a ransom for *all* men" (v. 6).

I have italicized above the four times the word "all" or "everyone" (Greek *panta*) appears in this paragraph. These four "alls" are connected. In this letter Paul is combatting a heresy (probably an incipient form of Gnosticism) which taught that only those belonging to a spiritual elite could be saved. In this paragraph Paul responds to this heresy and says salvation is for everyone, even for such unlikely candidates as earthly rulers. We know this because God desires all to be saved and Christ died for all. But this passage does not say that all will actually be saved.

Twice in this letter Paul warns Timothy to be faithful if he is hoping to find salvation in the end (4:16 ; 6:18, 19). Those warnings would not make sense if Paul did not leave a possibility of some not being saved in the end. We argue that 2:3, 4 says that God desires the salvation of all, but does not say that all will in fact be saved.

Second Peter 3:9 also expresses God's desire for the salvation of all: "The Lord . . . is patient with you, not wanting anyone to perish, but everyone to come to repentance." This verse comes in the middle of a description of "the Day of the Lord," when the earth will be destroyed, the judgment will take place, and the eternal states of the lost and the redeemed will be sealed. Verse 9 is Peter's answer to those who question why this day is being delayed. He says, "The Lord is not slow in keeping his promise, as some understand slowness." His delay is because "he is patient . . . not wanting anyone to perish but everyone to come to repentance." The desire that more would be saved causes him to delay the judgment. But Peter has already said that at "the day of judgment" there will be the "destruction of ungodly men" (v. 7).

So we cannot draw from an exegetical study of these texts the implication that all will be saved. But the universalist says that though this may not be an exegetical implication, it is a necessary theological implication. All things are possible with God. Therefore, if he desires the salvation of all, all will be saved. We will now consider this claim.

CAN GOD'S WISH BE FRUSTRATED?

Some have distinguished the desire of God for the salvation of mankind from the decree of God. According to this distinction, God desires all to be saved, but he has decreed that only those who exercise faith will in fact be saved. But the question is, can God's desire be frustrated?

The Scriptures teach that sometimes God does not do what he wishes to do because of the sinfulness of man. People defy God's will, and therefore only those who do the will of God are saved (see Matt. 7:21; 12:50; John 7:17; 1 John 2:17). Isaiah 65:12 says, "I will destine you for the sword, and you will all bend down for the slaughter; for I called but you did not answer, I spoke but you did not listen. You did evil in my sight and chose what displeases me." Jesus' lament over Jerusalem is very vivid: "O Jerusalem, Jerusalem, you who kill the prophets and stone those sent to you, how often I have longed to gather your children together, as a hen gathers her chicks under her wings, but you were not willing" (Matt. 23:37). "Jesus wanted to gather them together . . . but they did not want to be gathered together" (G. C. Berkouwer).[3]

ALL THINGS ARE POSSIBLE WITH GOD

Universalists say that the only way to reconcile God's inability to save all he desires to save and his omnipotence is to hold that all will be finally saved. John Hick says that one who rejects universalism must concede that God "is only limitedly sovereign."[4]

We respond by affirming that when the Bible says that all things are possible with God, it means that *all things are possible with God within the rules that God in his wisdom and sovereignty has set* as necessary for a good creation. One of these rules is that he will save only those who willingly come to him in faith.

When the rich young ruler left Jesus sorrowfully, Jesus remarked that it is extremely difficult for a rich person to enter the Kingdom. The disciples, bewildered by this statement, asked Jesus, "Who then can be saved?" Jesus replied, "With man this is impossible, but with God all things are possible" (Matt. 19:26). What Jesus was saying was that God can do the humanly impossible thing of saving a rich man. But the rich young man was not saved. This is because even though God can save the hardest heart, that heart must be willing to let God save it by exercising faith. The boundless saving power of God is limited by the way God ordained to save people—the way of faith.

The sovereign God has chosen to act only in ways that are compatible with his absolutely good nature. This is why, for example, the Bible says that God "cannot disown himself" (2 Tim. 2:13), that "it is impossible for God to lie" (Heb. 6:18), and that "God cannot be tempted by evil" (Jas. 1:13).

It may be objected that disowning himself, lying, and temptation by evil are things that God does not desire, whereas saving all people is something which he desires. We agree. But saving those who do not want to repent is not something that God desires to do. Doing that would be contrary to his standards of goodness.

But surely if God is all-wise and all-powerful, could he not have somehow made all people to believe in him? But if God did that, he would have to force himself on the impenitent. For salvation to be genuine, it should be willingly accepted. Human beings have a will, unlike robots. Salvation is essentially the establishing of a personal relationship by a free individual with his or her Creator. God takes the initiative and gives the strength to establish this relationship. But for the offer to be genuinely free, there should be the freedom to accept or reject it.

Universalist John Hick agrees with this. He says, "It seems

that there would be no point in the creation of finite persons unless they could be endowed with a degree of genuine freedom and independence over against their Maker. For only then could they be capable of authentic personal relationships with him."[5]

We showed in Chapter 4 that some people will be set in their way of rebellion to the end. The only way that God can bring such people to himself is by coercion. Origen had to concede this. He said there are those "whose conversion is in a certain degree demanded and extorted."[6] Jerry Walls pertinently asks, "If God is finally willing to convert men by coercion we may legitimately wonder why he gave them real freedom in the first place, since so much suffering has resulted from the abuse of freedom."[7]

Our conclusion is that God's omnipotence means that he can do all that is good, however impossible doing that may seem to us. It is not good to save the impenitent. Therefore he will not do that. We can go so far as to say that he does not wish to save those who have spurned salvation. To save them he would have to act contrary to his nature of goodness and also have to deprive them of their humanity by the use of coercion.

CHAPTER NINE

IS GOD BEING JUST
AND FAIR?

No worse insult could be offered to Christ and no blasphemy of God could go deeper than this. God's name has been libelled beyond belief even by those who sincerely think they know him, love him and serve him. Yet an idol they serve, not the God of the Christian faith.[1]

That is what Nels Ferre thinks about the doctrine of eternal hell! He says this doctrine is "subjustice and sublove." The justice and love of God are the topics of this and the next chapter.

THE BIBLICAL EMPHASIS ON THE JUSTICE
OF JUDGMENT

The Bible is keenly aware of the importance of the relationship between judgment and justice. Wilbur M. Smith points out that "judgment is hardly ever spoken of in the Word of God unless at the same time it is characterized as *righteous* judgment."[2] He lists twenty texts where the judgment is described as being righteous.

He starts with the question Abraham asked in Genesis 18:25 as he pondered the impending judgment of Sodom: "Will not the Judge of all the earth do right?" and ends with the cry of the angel in Revelation 16:5: "You are just in these judgments, you who are and who were, the Holy One, because you have so judged."

The NIV often uses the word "justice" where the old *Authorised Version* used "righteousness." Leon Morris says, "Where in English we have two word-groups to express the concepts of 'justice' and 'righteousness' . . . in Hebrew and Greek . . . the one word does duty for both concepts."[3] There has been a lot of discussion about the meaning of this word-group (*dikaios, dikaiosune*, etc. in Greek). Two meanings of "custom" and "right" seem to have been associated with it from its earliest use. Morris says that, as used in the first century, "these words do not indicate something arbitrary, but something in conformity with some standard of right."[4]

So when the Bible associates righteousness or justice with God's judgment, it means that it conforms to the way God always acts. It is his nature to judge sin. As A. H. Strong says, "All arbitrariness is excluded here. . . . God can cease to demand purity and to punish sin only when he ceases to be holy, that is, only when he ceases to be God."[5]

Now these judgments which are described in the Bible as being just were very severe. Many today recoil with horror over them. They include the destruction of Sodom and some of the judgments described in Revelation (16:5, 7; 19:2, 11). But they are in keeping with God's good nature.

People today find the biblical portrait of judgment so repulsive because, as an American proverb puts it, some believe that God is too good to damn anyone, while others believe that man is too good for any God to damn. Let us now look at these two problems that people have with eternal punishment.

CONTEMPORARY VIEWS OF HUMAN NATURE

G. K. Chesterton has said that it is surprising that people have rejected the doctrine of original sin because it is the only doctrine which can be empirically verified. All we need to do to see what a mess man has made of this world is to read a newspaper. Yet this is the age of the human potential movement that glories in the possibilities of human ability. A poll done for *Newsweek* magazine by the Gallup organization in December 1988 found that 77 percent of Americans believe there is a heaven, and 76 percent think they have a good or excellent chance of getting there.[6] Such is the confidence of this godless generation.

The New Age movements which are flourishing in the West proclaim that all humans are essentially divine. This reflects the traditional Hindu concept which finds it difficult to visualize the existence of such a thing as evil. And if humans are essentially divine, how could they be consigned to an eternal hell? They see man as progressing through many lives towards the goal of total fusion with the divine.

Buddhism prides itself in being a system that needs no help from a divine savior. They believe that people have the ability to strive toward their goal of *Nirvana*. Many schools of psychology have taught people to avoid thinking about the idea of sin because it is said to cause an unhealthy sense of guilt in them. The noted American psychiatrist Karl Menninger responded to this attitude in his book, *Whatever Became of Sin?*[7] Even some preachers have been influenced by the fact that human beings enjoy being told how good they are. This is seen in the many sermons that affirm people and say how good they are, while ignoring sin and repentance.

This confidence in human ability has resulted in a soft attitude towards sin and unbelief even among Christians. When the young British missionary Henry Martyn saw a worship ceremony at a Hindu temple in India, he said, "This excited more horror in me than I can express. . . . I thought that if I had words I would preach to the multitudes all day if I lost my life for it."[8] He was reflecting the attitude of Paul, who was "greatly distressed" when he saw the idols in Athens (Acts 17:16). Today, however, many Christians express admiration and even approval for the religious dedication of non-Christians.

When Ezra found that God's people had compromised their faith by marrying unbelievers, this was his response:

> When I heard this, I tore my tunic and cloak, pulled hair from my head and beard and sat down appalled. . . . Then, at the evening sacrifice, I rose from my self-abasement, with my tunic and cloak torn, and fell on my knees with my hands spread out to the Lord my God and prayed. (Ezra 9:3-6)

How alien all this biblical way of thinking is to many Christians today. This is why many find the doctrine of judgment unpalatable. The problem lies not in the doctrine of judgment; it lies within us! Robert Mounce has said that "all caricatures of God which ignore his intense hatred for sin reveal more about man than about God."[9]

Paul has some drastic things to say about the sinfulness of the human race. In Romans 3:10-18 he gathers together an impressive array of quotations to drive home this point:

> There is no one righteous, not even one;
> there is no one who understands,
> no one who seeks God.
> All have turned away,
> they have together become worthless;
> there is no one who does good,
> not even one.
> Their throats are open graves;
> their tongues practice deceit.
> The poison of vipers is on their lips.

Their mouths are full of cursing and bitterness.
Their feet are swift to shed blood;
ruin and misery mark their ways,
and the way of peace they do not know.

Paul climaxes this description with a summary statement of what the basic sin of humanity is: "There is no fear of God before their eyes" (v. 18). He concludes that because of this sinfulness ". . . every mouth may be silenced and the whole world held accountable to God" (v. 19). On the Day of Judgment the lost will agree that they deserve to be punished.

But why is the refusal to have a "fear of God before their eyes" such a serious sin, meriting so great a punishment? In the next few pages we will use a somewhat circuitous route to answer this question.

THE GLORY OF GOD: LIFE'S MOST IMPORTANT FACTOR

The major affirmation we will defend below is that *the refusal to hear God, which is the heart of unbelief, is ultimately an affront to the glory of God. And to affront the glory of God is the most serious crime that one could commit.*

The Bible teaches the absolute importance of God's glory in terms of the purpose and goal of the created universe. In this purpose and goal of creation lies the key to the meaning of life. So, *manifesting the glory of God is the great end to which creation eagerly looks forward.* Psalm 72:19 prays, "May the whole earth be filled with his glory." Isaiah 40:5 anticipates the day when "the glory of the Lord will be revealed, and all mankind together will see it." Habakkuk 2:14 describes this day thus: "For the earth will be filled with the knowledge of the glory of the Lord, as the waters cover the sea" (see also Isa. 66:18).

Thus the faithful are asked in the present age to "declare his glory among the nations" (Ps. 96:3). Isaiah 66:19 looks forward to the great day when God "will send [preachers] to the nations . . . and to the distant islands that have not heard of [God's] fame or seen [his] glory." And this will be their message: "They will proclaim my glory among the nations."

Why is the glory of God so crucial to understanding the meaning of life? The Hebrew word for "glory," *kabōd*, has the basic idea of "worthiness." When used of God, it denotes his greatness, character and worth. When we say that we saw the glory of God, we mean that we saw what he is like.

This glory is necessary for the welfare of the universe because God is intimately involved with the creation. He is not only the Creator of this universe, he is also its sustainer (Deut. 30:20; Job 12:10; Dan. 5:23b; Acts 17:28; Col. 1:17b; Heb. 1:3b). God is necessary for life to go on. Without him, this universe would fall into nothingness. Not only does he sustain it—he has made it so that it finds its meaning only as it conforms to his will. To conform to the will of God is to express the nature of God on earth, which is the same as glorifying God. This is why the Bible says the creation finds a clue to its purpose in the glory of God. When it glorifies God, it is brought into harmony with the nature of its sustainer.

So for the welfare of the world the most important thing that can happen is to maintain this glory. Therefore, maintaining his glory is the most benevolent thing God can do for this world. This is why *God is often described in the Bible as acting to preserve and enhance his glory or his name.* If that were done by a human, it would be regarded as selfishness. But when God preserves and enhances his glory, he is giving the world its only source of real goodness.

Daniel P. Fuller has made an impressive list of the instances in the Bible where God is said to act to enhance his glory (or name) on earth.[10] God created people for his own glory (Isa. 43:7); he redeems people and forgives their sins for the sake of his name (Ps. 25:11; 79:9; 1 John 2:12). He guides his people in the ways of righteousness for his name's sake (Ps. 23:3; 31:3). Even though Israel sinned in wanting a king, God sent word through Samuel that "for the sake of his great name the Lord will not reject his people" (1 Sam. 12:22). Isaiah 48:9, 11 is "perhaps the most striking of all passages" (Fuller):

> For my own name's sake I delay my wrath; for the sake of my praise I hold it back from you. . . . For my own sake, for my own sake, I do this. How can I let myself be defamed? I will not yield my glory to another.

In the Bible *judgment is also an act which enhances God's glory.* When Aaron's two sons were destroyed by fire because they offered unauthorized fire before the Lord, Moses explained to the grieved Aaron that this incident was an illustration of the way God preserves his glory. Moses says, "This is what the Lord spoke when he said: 'Among those who approach me I will show myself holy; in the sight of all the people I will be honored'" (Lev. 10:3).

Revelation records the inhabitants of heaven praising God for his judgments because they have affirmed the justice and glory of God, which had been challenged by the actions of the wicked (6:10; 11:17, 18; 16:5-7; 18:20; 19:1-3). Revelation 19:1-3 says,

> After this I heard what sounded like the roar of a great multitude in heaven shouting: "Hallelujah! Salvation and glory and power belong to our God, for true and just are his judgments. He has condemned the great prostitute who corrupted the earth by her adulteries. He has avenged on her the blood of his servants." And again they shouted: "Hallelujah!"

The heavenly multitude praises God for his judgment because judgment is the most appropriate response to affronts to God's glory. To challenge God's glory is to challenge all that is good about creation. Therefore, judging sinners not only enhances the glory of God, it also restores goodness to creation. This is why we say that *judgment is essentially a benevolent act.*

Let me now summarize what I have argued for in a somewhat complicated way.

1. When the Bible speaks of God as acting righteously, it means that he acts in ways that conform to his nature.

2. To act in ways that conform to his nature is the same as acting to enhance his glory.

3. So when the Bible says God's judgment is righteous, it means judgment enhances his glory.

4. Judgment enhances his glory by responding adequately to affronts to his glory.

5. Because acting to enhance his glory is essentially a benevolent act which seeks the best for creation, judgment too is a benevolent act.

THE SERIOUSNESS OF UNBELIEF

But is unbelief such a serious affront to God's glory as to merit eternal punishment?

We all agree that in a society there are crimes that are of varying intensities of seriousness. The criterion for judging the seriousness of a crime is how much the offense affects others and therefore the honor of the state, whose task it is to enhance the welfare of its citizens. A parking violation is considered a minor offense, and in most countries a light fine is charged for it. A robbery is considered more serious. The harm done through it is more than that done through the inconvenience caused by a parking violation. Even more serious is murder. But the most serious offense is treason. That is a crime of national proportions affecting not just a few individuals but the security and welfare of a whole nation.

Dr. Fuller gives the execution of Vidkun Quisling in 1945 in

Norway as an example of how governments regard the seriousness of treason. Norway had abolished the death penalty in 1905. From 1940 to 1945 Quisling was governor of Norway, and he aided the Nazis in bleeding his country. After the war, when Quisling was tried, it was determined that there was no punishment severe enough in their laws to adequately respond to his treachery and restore the honor of this nation that had been degraded through his actions. So they reinstituted the death penalty and applied it to Quisling.

The Bible presents unbelief as such an act of treason. Romans 8:7 says that "the sinful mind is hostile to God." The sin of Adam and Eve was not just another act of disobedience against God. The Serpent told them that by eating of the fruit they would "be like God, knowing good and evil" (Gen. 3:5). Whereas earlier they had looked to God for guidance as to what is good and what is evil, now they would make that choice. They would be independent of God. As the Serpent put it, they would "be like God."

Looking back to the choice of humanity to assert its independence against God, Paul said,

> Although they knew God, they neither glorified him as God nor gave thanks to him . . . they became fools and exchanged the glory of the immortal God for images. . . . They . . . worshiped and served created things rather than the Creator. (Rom. 1:21, 22, 23, 25)

So unbelief is not only acting in a way that displeases God, it is rejecting the constituted government of the universe. It is seeking to put in its place another government. Unbelief rejects the idea that the glory of God is what is needed for the welfare of the universe and instead seeks to glory in a created object. This is why the Apostle Paul and Henry Martyn recoiled in horror as they were confronted by the idolatry in Athens and India. God himself expressed his horror over unbelief through Jeremiah in a memorable statement:

> "Has any nation ever changed its gods? . . . But my people have exchanged their Glory for worthless idols. Be appalled at this, O heavens, and shudder with great horror," declares the Lord. "My people have committed two sins: They have forsaken me, the spring of living water, and have dug their own cisterns, broken cisterns that cannot hold water." (Jer. 2:11-13)

The above reasoning shows why Paul exclaimed that there is no one who is righteous (Rom. 3:10). Even the so-called righteous acts of an unbeliever are part of his rebellion against the way of God. When a religious person does a good deed to acquire merit and so contribute to his or her salvation, that person is declaring war on the glory of God by attempting to find salvation independently of God.

Unbelief, then, is an open act of rebellion against the glory of God. The glory of God is the only means for the welfare of this universe. Whereas individual acts of sin, such as stealing and violence, violate the system of laws of the universe, unbelief is a rebellion against the system itself. This is why it is so serious. And this is why it merits a punishment of such enormity. For the preservation of the glory of creation and therefore for the benefit of its inhabitants God must respond to this affront to his glory with adequate severity.

Jonathan Edwards (1703-1758) has made famous the idea that because sin against the infinite God is an infinite thing, the punishment for that act also must be infinite. Universalists like Ferre object to this by saying that "only the infinite could sin infinitely." A human is not infinite; "infinite sin is therefore impossible."[11] Edwards would respond that sin against God is infinite, not because we do it, but because it is sin against the infinite God. While I am not in a position to accept or reject this argument, I present it as one way a great theologian explained the eternity of punishment.[12]

DEGREES OF PUNISHMENT

We have shown in Chapter 2 that the Bible teaches that in hell there will be degrees of punishment. This is another key to understanding the justice of judgment.

This principle applies in the case of those who have not heard the gospel. Their judgment will not be for the failure to respond to a gospel they never had an opportunity to hear. Romans 2 teaches that they will be judged according to the light they received. But it also teaches that no one lives according to the light they receive. People choose to be disobedient to that light, and God is just in punishing them.[13]

However, their responsibility is much less than those who knowingly rejected the gospel. We may call this diminished responsibility. They are guilty, but their guilt is less. Hebrews 10:26-31 says that some will be punished "much more severely." That means that some will receive a much lighter punishment than others.

This principle would also apply to people from backgrounds that are not conducive to growing up in the ways of God. The son of a prostitute who grows up in the slums surrounded by crime and violence has a lesser chance of responding to the gospel than one from a healthy Christian home. His responsibility is diminished. Every person who comes into the world receives some light (John 1:9). So every person, however bad his background may be, is responsible for rejecting the light that he received. All are lost and deserve to be punished. But the punishment on those with diminished responsibility will be much less than on those with greater responsibility.

It seems to me that the horrible pictures of torment given in the Bible are particularly applied to those with great responsibility.

We do not know what form the punishment of those with diminished responsibility will take. What we do know is that it is eternal and characterized by what is associated with the absence of light and joy. It will be a time of regret and of suffering in hell. We cannot say what form that will take. We leave that in the hands of the Judge of all the earth who will do what is right (Gen. 18:25).

CHAPTER TEN

WRATH VERSUS GOD'S LOVE

How can God send people to an eternal hell? I tried to answer that question in the previous chapter. Some still object by saying that the scriptural teaching of love must eliminate the idea of an eternal hell. We said that Nels Ferre rejected the doctrine of eternal hell because it was "subjustice" and "sublove." We looked at the subjustice accusation in the last chapter. We will now look at the sublove accusation.

There are two issues that usually cause people to conclude that the scriptural teaching of the love of God contradicts the idea of an eternal hell. The first is based on the idea that the message of the Bible is essentially a message of love. Eternal punishment is said to contradict this message. We will deal with this viewpoint in the next chapter.

The second issue arises out of an understanding of the nature of God as loving. John said, "God is love" (l John 4:8). Love is said to be the supreme characteristic of God. Everything else about God must take a subordinate position. Some even claim that God's wrath is an element of his love. If so, his wrath must always act to fulfill an aim of love. Therefore, what is known as eternal punishment should result in salvation.

We will now show that the Bible does not warrant the subordination of the other qualities of God to love.

WRATH DIVORCED FROM THE NATURE OF GOD

The question about the relationship between God's nature and wrath has been a problem right from the early years of the church. In the second century A.D. Marcion said that the wrath described in the Old Testament was alien to the nature of the loving God who is the Father of Jesus Christ. So, in order to accommodate the Old Testament teaching, he spoke of a different god, not the Father of Jesus, who was a vindictive god. Far above this vindictive god is the "unknown God" who is Love. Marcion had to reckon with the fact that wrath is mentioned in the New Testament also. But he tried to circumvent this problem by dropping many books from the New Testament. He ended up with his famous canon consisting of Paul's letters and the Gospel by Paul's companion, Luke. But we know that even Marcion's hero, Paul, had a lot to say about wrath.

In the last century influential theologians like F. D. E. Schleiermacher and A. Ritschl helped to spearhead a movement away from considering wrath an essential part of God's nature. In this century the well-known British New Testament scholar C. H. Dodd popularized the idea that wrath is retained in the New Testament "not to describe the attitude of God to man, but to describe the inevitable process of retribution."[1] This was also advocated more recently by another British scholar, A. T. Hanson, who says,

> There can be little doubt that for Paul the impersonal character of the wrath was important; it relieved him of the necessity of attributing wrath directly to God, it transformed

wrath from an attribute of God into the name for the process, which sinners bring upon themselves.[2]

He says that wrath "does not describe an attitude of God but a condition of men."[3]

According to Dodd, "Wrath is the effect of human sin: mercy is not the effect of human goodness, but it is inherent in the character of God."[4] If one were to pursue this reasoning further, he would have to conclude that God would not permit a principle which operates outside of himself (wrath) to override something which is inherent to his character (mercy). Because wrath could never overcome love, no one could be permanently punished. That is, all humanity must be saved. Dodd argues for universalism in the commentary on Romans where he propounds this idea of wrath.[5]

Many Christians today find it difficult to accept the biblical teaching of eternal punishment because they consider wrath to be uncharacteristic of God.

THE BIBLICAL UNDERSTANDING OF GOD'S NATURE

The biblical picture of God is very different from what we have just described. The New Testament portrait of Jesus bears this out.[6] I will never forget a ten-year-old student in a Sunday school class I taught asking me very earnestly, "If Jesus was a good man, how could he have acted the way he did at the temple [of Jerusalem when he cleansed it]?" He simply could not reconcile that outburst of wrath with his idea of the goodness of God.

We see a similar outburst of wrath when Jesus denounced "the cities in which most of his miracles had been performed, because they did not repent." After pronouncing "Woe!" to Korazin and Bethsaida and expressing the seriousness of their sin, he says, "It will be more bearable for Tyre and Sidon on the day of judgment than for you." To Capernaum he says, "It will be more bearable for Sodom on the day of judgment than for you" (Matt. 11:20-24).

Note that Jesus not only endorses the Old Testament judgments upon Tyre, Sidon and Sodom, which many consider uncharacteristic of the God of the New Testament, but he predicts an even worse fate for these unrepentant cities.

Christ's harsh words to the Pharisees are the most vivid of all. Matthew 23 contains a sustained attack on them that is surprising even to those who have no problems with accepting wrath as an inherent part of God's nature. This is where we get the "seven woes." We hear from the Savior's lips such statements as, "You hypocrites," which appears six times, and "blind guides," which appears twice. Other expressions about blindness appear three more times. "You are like whitewashed tombs," he says, "which look beautiful on the outside but on the inside are full of dead men's bones and everything unclean" (v. 27). Verse 33 talks about judgment: "You snakes! You brood of vipers! How will you escape being condemned to hell?" Such evidence leads Gustav Stahlin to conclude that "wrath is an integral characteristic of the Jesus of the Gospels."[7]

In this same chapter, after the seven woes, Jesus exclaims, "O Jerusalem, Jerusalem, you who kill the prophets and stone those sent to you, how often I have longed to gather your children together, as a hen gathers her chicks under her wings . . ." (v. 37). It is significant that such a tender expression of love should come alongside one of Christ's most severe outbursts of wrath. That is possible only because wrath and love are equally part of Christ's nature.

In this instance, however, the love is rejected. Just after the tender expression come the words, ". . . but you were not willing." That unwillingness results in God acting in wrath despite his expression of love. So the next verse says, "Look, your house is left to you desolate." G. C. Berkouwer comments on this text that "in the revelation of Christ the wrath of God is revealed when the lost are sought and do not want to be found."[8] The same God who seeks people in love responds with wrath toward those who reject him.

Dodd and Hanson say that in Paul's epistles wrath is not presented as a part of the nature of God. The following texts show that this claim is unfounded:

Romans 1:18: "The *wrath of God* is being revealed from heaven against all the godlessness and wickedness of men. . . ."

Romans 2:5, 6: "But because of your stubbornness and your unrepentant heart, you are storing up *wrath* against yourself for the day of *God's wrath*, when his righteous judgment will be revealed. God 'will give to each person according to what he has done.'" Note that the wrath does not happen automatically. God is the one who gives the punishment.

Romans 3:5, 6: ". . . what shall we say? That God is unjust in bringing *his wrath* on us? . . . Certainly not! If that were so, how could God judge the world?"

Romans 9:22: "What if God, choosing to show *his wrath* and make his power known, bore with great patience the objects of *his wrath*—prepared for destruction?"

Texts could be given from the other epistles and the book of Revelation too. As we saw above, Paul speaks of "God, choosing to show his wrath . . ." (Rom. 9:22). The word translated "choosing" is the word *thelo*, which is usually translated "to wish, want, desire, will or like." It clearly presents God's involvement in the wrath. This is the word that Paul uses when he declares that God "wants all men to be saved and come to a knowledge of the truth" (1 Tim. 2:4). If we were to present the teachings of Romans 9:22 and 1 Timothy 2:4 together, we would say that the same God who desires to save all people also desires to show his wrath upon those who reject his loving offer.

The evidence given above shows that we must put wrath and love on an equal footing as being intrinsic to God's nature. While the Bible says that God is love, it does not say that God is *only love*.

It also says that God is righteous, holy, and angry at man's sin. Love is probably the most attractive aspect of God's nature. But we cannot understand what it means if we divorce it from the other aspects. We must behold both the kindness and the severity of God (Rom. 11:22).

God's kindness and severity are best demonstrated in the death of Jesus. When God in his love provided a way for humanity's forgiveness, he gave expression to his wrath against sin in all its severity. In his book *The Apostolic Preaching of the Cross*,[9] Leon Morris has shown convincingly that this is the meaning of the word "propitiation" that is used in the New Testament to describe the sacrifice of Christ (Rom. 3:25; 1 John 2:2; 4:10). At the cross God showed that his love cannot act in contradiction to his righteous wrath against sin.

WHAT IS WRATH?

We face a problem when describing God's wrath because our idea of wrath has been influenced by expressions of selfish anger that we have seen on earth. Rarely do we see a person being angry without compromising love. What we usually see is an outburst of uncontrolled, selfish passion which does more harm than good. Leon Morris says, "Nobody wants to attribute to God the weakness we know so well from human anger."[10]

Yet even on the human plane we see the need for the combination of love and wrath. Sometimes when I don't get angry at some wrong which I am confronted with, I realize that this refusal to be angry is a sin. It is an expression of my fallenness, not of my saintliness. Sometimes we hear people say about a teacher, "He's such a saint—he never gets angry, whatever his students may do." That teacher may be guilty of the sin of condoning wrong and may thus be adversely affecting the discipline of the school and the healthy development of his students!

What we are saying is that sternness is necessary for the stability of the world. Evil must be dealt with. Evildoers must know that what they do is wrong. Not to do so is to insult goodness and make it worthless. A child who has not been disciplined at home is usually an insecure child. He may proudly proclaim to his friends that he can get away with anything. But in his innermost heart there is that nagging feeling that he was not important enough to his parents to have elicited some response for his wrong action. If God did not react with wrath to man's sin, that sin would not be significant and therefore man would not be significant.

Leon Morris has said, "We sometimes find among men a love which is untempered by a sterner side, and this we call not love but sentimentality." He says, "It is not such that the Bible thinks of when it speaks of the love of God, but rather love which is so jealous of the loved one that it blazes out in fiery wrath against everything that is evil."[11] This is what the Bible means when it speaks of wrath.

THE RESULTS OF REMOVING WRATH FROM THEOLOGY

When we remove wrath from our understanding of the essential nature of God, heresy results. Carl Henry has said, "The subordination of divine righteousness to divine love leads to arbitrary conceptions of *agape* in which God's judgment and wrath do not come to full scriptural expression, and from which grossly unbiblical consequences are still deduced."[12]

Henry is talking about the type of deduction made by Nels Ferre when he claimed that because love is ultimate, all must be saved.[13] It is because of such deductions that so many people are having problems with the doctrine of eternal punishment today. They find it difficult to accommodate this in their belief-system which views God as being "pure love." When wrath is given its place as equally a part of God's nature, we can accommodate the belief that the God who saves some eternally also punishes others eternally.

Another result of ignoring God's wrath is that we will have problems in comprehending the meaning of salvation. If we don't understand the immensity of God's hatred for sin, then we won't understand the immensity of God's mercy either. We would not realize what a terrible state God saved us from. Therefore we would not realize how great is our salvation.

R. V. G. Tasker in an influential booklet on wrath, written almost forty years ago, quoted F. C. Synge as saying, "Those who perceive only the love of God avert their eyes from the uncongenial doctrine of the wrath of God. But in eliminating the wrath or disgrace of God they have also eliminated the grace of God. Where there is no fear there can be no rescue. Where there is no condemnation there can be no acquittal." Tasker himself writes, "By seeking to eliminate hell we must in effect also eliminate heaven."[14]

HOW UNIVERSALISTS HANDLE THE BIBLE

We have already shown that even universalists concede that the Bible teaches eternal punishment. Yet they reject this doctrine. In this chapter we will look at how universalists explain the contradiction between what they believe and what the Bible teaches about the final destiny of the lost.

HANDLING THE TWO GROUPS OF TEXTS

We will first examine how universalists handle the two groups of texts said to teach universal salvation and eternal punishment.

Scriptures Taken out of Context

Universalists appeal to numerous texts which, they claim, teach that all will be saved in the end. We have already discussed these texts and showed that they do not proclaim this hope at all. These texts have been taken out of their context and understood in a way contrary to the intention of the biblical authors. The context helps decide against a universalistic interpretation.

Picking and Choosing Scriptures

We have already said that most universalists agree that some texts teach that some will be irreversibly lost. But they reject this body of Scripture in favor of what they regard as the universalistic passages. Some, like C. Ryder Smith, choose to remain agnostic about this issue as they keep the two bodies of supposedly contrasting texts "in unresolved tension."[1]

Both these positions are unsatisfactory for those who seek to be biblical in their approach to truth. The so-called universalistic passages can be explained in non-universalistic ways, and have been explained this way by the vast majority of biblical scholars throughout the history of the church. On the other hand even universalists agree that the passages teaching eternal punishment cannot be interpreted in any other way.

This means that those who claim that the Scriptures teach universalism rest their case upon the doubtful interpretations of some texts while rejecting the undoubted interpretations of other texts. This lays one open to the charge of misrepresenting the Word of God.

The Bodies of Scripture Used

Most of the texts used in support of universalism appear in the writings of John and Paul, which those with a liberal view of biblical criticism consider historically inferior and not accurately representing the thinking of Christ. N. T. Wright calls this an "odd inversion . . . of the old liberal position."[2] Note that the majority of universalists subscribe to this liberal approach to Scripture.

On the other hand, many of the texts teaching eternal punishment come from the Synoptic Gospels, which liberal criticism considers to be more accurate. Despite this, they hold that the universalistic texts in John and Paul represent the heart of Christ's teaching, whereas the punishment texts in the Synoptics have been taken over from the contemporary Jewish environment.

John Hick says the Gospel texts about final judgment are not the authentic words of Jesus.[3] Yet, as Richard Bauckham points out, even if one were to stringently use the "generally accepted criteria of authenticity . . . the warning of final judgment cannot be eliminated from Jesus' authentic words."[4] That is, they appear in sections of the Synoptics which even liberal critics consider to be authentic. This points to the weakness of the universalists' appeal to the Scriptures.

REINTERPRETING THE PREDICTIONS

Sometimes the predictions about eternal punishment in the Bible are given interpretations that are different from the usual way the texts are understood.

Unfulfilled Threats?

John Hick regards these predictions as threats that will not be fulfilled. He says, "It may well be true that at a given point within the temporal process, unless you repent you will surely perish." If a person persists in "permanent non-repentance," eternal punishment will be the result. But he says that no one will remain in permanent non-repentance: "In the end all will turn from their wickedness and live."[5] So while eternal punishment is a theoretical possibility, it is a practical impossibility.

To explain how the final repentance of all humanity will take place, Hick propounds an ingenious theory of purgatorial reincarnation, where an exact replica of the person reincarnates in a different world.[6] This theory perhaps has a closer affinity to the *Tibetan Book of the Dead* and other Buddhist literature than to the Bible.

To take the predictions about eternal judgment as threats that will not be fulfilled is to change the unmistakably evident intention of these statements and thus do serious injustice to them. What does one do with Jesus' statement that "anyone who speaks against the Holy Spirit will not be forgiven, either in this age or in the age to come" (Matt. 12:32)? By relegating predictions to the status of unfulfilled threats Hick is bringing into question the integrity of Christ. Only a dishonest person would make hollow predictions that he knows would never take place.

To Be Interpreted Subjectively?

Nels Ferre says that the New Testament is "the existential source-book (not the literal textbook) of Christian doctrine." He says that doctrines like that of eternal punishment are found in the Bible "because preaching is existential."[7] So without taking prophecies literally, we must see what pastoral lesson can be gleaned from them. For example, we preach about the terrors of hell so that sinners will find out that it is a fearful thing to fall into the hands of the living God and so repent of their sins. What is important is that the sinner repents, and not whether there is such a thing as an eternal hell or not.

Bishop Robinson says that the eschatological assertions in the Bible are expressed in the form of what he calls "myths."[8] He says they "are neither inerrant prophecies of the future nor pious guess work." Rather, "they are necessary transpositions into the key of the hereafter of knowledge of God and his relation to man given in the revelatory encounter of present historical event."[9] These eschatological statements tell us something about the experiences of the biblical authors. As such they have relevance to our present experience.

Bishop Robinson cites Christ's answer to the disciples' question, "Lord, are only a few people going to be saved?" (Luke 13:23). Jesus answered, "Make every effort to enter through the narrow door, because many, I tell you, will try to enter and will not be able to" (v. 24). From this Robinson points out that Jesus refused to give an objective answer to that question. Rather he insisted "on recalling each man to take his stand as 'subject' before the choice that confronts him." The message of this verse, then, is that to the one who is in the position of deciding to enter the Kingdom, "the door is narrow."[10] So to questions regarding the destiny of mankind the Bible gives practical answers that affect the reader in the present.

But does this approach do justice to the text? If one were to read this passage without being colored by this existential or subjective approach to the Bible, he would immediately see that Jesus' answer to this question includes some definite predictions. There are a total of eight verbs in the future tense in verses 24 to 30. These include:

> . . . many, I tell you, *will try* to enter and *will not be able to*. (v. 24)

> There *will be* weeping there, and gnashing of teeth, when you see Abraham, Isaac and Jacob and all the prophets in the kingdom of God, but you yourselves thrown out. (v. 28)

> People will *come* from east and west and north and south, and *will take their places* at the feast in the kingdom of God. (v. 29)

Those who use this approach can ignore this undoubtedly predictive element in this passage only by making up their minds before going to the Scripture that it does not contain objective prophecies. When they face these prophecies they apply a radical interpretive device so as to divest them of their predictive element. What we are left with, then, is not what the Bible says about the future, but what the universalists would like it to say!

Biblical Christians agree that the primary aim of the prophetic passages in the Bible is to help the readers in their daily life, but they don't divest them of their predictive element.

If a parent threatens to punish a child severely after he did certain wrong things, but had no intention of carrying out those threats, we would regard that parent as untruthful. The children would lose their respect for the parent who used a means that was not quite correct in order to make them act in a certain way. If the Creator of the universe practiced this type of inconsistency, the world would be a terribly insecure place to live in, especially for those who follow him. But God is faithful. His Son urged his followers, "Simply let your 'Yes' be 'Yes,' and your 'No,' 'No'" (Matt. 5:37). If that is the type of conversation he recommended, we can be assured that when he himself predicted something, he really meant it.

UNWARRANTED ASSUMPTIONS

It has already become evident that the desire of the universalists to prove their point has led them to inadequate approaches to biblical texts. This is particularly evident in some of the assumptions that universalists make while arguing their case.

Leaps in Argumentation

It is surprising to see how people who are otherwise meticulous scholars get so careless and jump to unwarranted conclusions when they deal with the fate of the lost. They say, for example, that because the Bible states that Christ is the Savior of the world, everyone in the world must be saved; or because the Bible portrays God as being loving, he must save everyone in the world.

In jumping from the biblical affirmation to the theological affirmation of universalism some necessary steps have been left out. Possible implications are made into necessary implications. Because

God is love it is possible to imply that he will save all. But we must go back to the source of our information about God—the Bible— to see whether this is a valid implication. When we do this, we find this implication to be wrong.

Instead of following this procedure, the universalists have taken a principle from a passage and absolutized it, and then made implications from that principle without further reference to the Scriptures. They have taken the Apostle John's affirmation that Jesus is the Savior of the world (John 1:29; 4:42; 12:47) and implied from this that all people will be saved.[11] This latter implication is directly contradicted in other parts of John. So John is made into a theological schizophrenic, a Dr. Jekyll and Mr. Hyde, making two contradictory statements, sometimes in the same paragraph.

A Biased Approach to the Biblical Data

Sometimes universalists make universalism a necessary starting-point for study, which provides almost absolute guidelines for interpretation. John Hick says, "In wrestling with the problem of evil I had concluded that any viable Christian theodicy[12] *must affirm* the ultimate salvation of all God's creatures."[13] Reverent Bible students should arrive at their conclusions only after studying the Scriptures, and they should revise their biases if Scripture contradicts them.

Nels Ferre makes a similar procedural error. After mentioning the supposed universalistic texts of the Bible, he says, "All such verses . . . are as nothing in comparison to the message of the New Testament." This total message is what Ferre calls "the logic of sovereign love." That is, "God would have all to be saved and with God all things are possible."[14] Elsewhere he says, "On the grounds of our total analysis of truth, moreover, our existential ultimate requires that all be saved, or else Agape is not ultimate."[15] Ferre concedes that the Bible teaches eternal punishment,[16] but that data is made subservient to his "total message of the Bible."

John Hick says we cannot be sure how exactly to interpret the word "eternal" (*aionios*) as it is used for punishment in the Bible. But he solves this problem by saying that "the textual evidence must be interpreted in the light of wider considerations drawn from Jesus' teaching as a whole." He concludes, "If we see as the heart of this teaching the message of active and divine sovereign love, we shall find incredible and even blasphemous the idea that God plans to inflict perpetual torture on any of his children."[17]

But is sovereign love the total message of the Scriptures? A. Pink reminds us that "there are *more* references in Scripture to the anger, fury and wrath of God than there are to his love and tenderness."[18] It has often been pointed out that in the recorded statements of Jesus there are more references to hell than to heaven. This does not mean that the doctrines of wrath and hell are more important than the doctrines of love and heaven. But it does require that the doctrines of wrath and hell play a significant role in determining the "total message" of the Bible and that this message must not contradict these doctrines. Ferre and Hick have failed to do this in their formulation of the total message. They have let the message of love cancel off the message of wrath and hell. The universalist idea of the whole contradicts such a significant portion of the parts that it simply cannot be regarded as a legitimate representation of the whole.

The type of thing universalists do with the wrath passages happens often. We often remember and emphasize only those parts of a passage which we find pleasing to us. Some of the popular Psalms often have the love of God and the wrath of God placed side by side. But usually when we think of these Psalms we only think of the love sections. If we read them publicly in a worship service, we sometimes conveniently leave out the verses that talk of wrath because we decide that they are not in harmony with the spirit of the service.

Recently I had an assignment of writing down a one- or two-sentence summary of the book of Hosea. From previous readings of this book I felt I knew what this summary would be even before reading it: "God's unchanging love for Israel." But when I sat down to read the book, I found that there was a lot about sin and judgment in it. Even though I had read through Hosea many times before, I did not remember that aspect as being a significant part of its message. This must not have been as inspiring and attractive as the emphasis on love. So my mind had chosen to ignore it.

When we ignore those parts of Scripture which we find unpleasant, we will end up with an understanding of the message of the Scriptures that has no place for wrath and hell.

THE FEAR OF RESTRICTING GOD'S FREEDOM

One of the main reasons why Karl Barth decided to take "no position for or against" universalism[19] was the fear that if he committed himself one way or the other he would be denying God's freedom to do as he pleases. He says:

> The intention and power of God in relation to the whole world and all men are always his intention and power—an intention and power which we cannot control and the limits of which we cannot arbitrarily restrict or change.[20]

Barth's point is that God will do as he chooses, and we have no right to make pronouncements as to whether all will be saved or not. Barth must be lauded for his emphasis on the sovereignty of God. But if the sovereign God has disclosed to humanity what he will do, then the appropriate response to his sovereignty is to believe what he has revealed. God has revealed unmistakably in the Scriptures that there will be some who will be lost eternally.

Therefore, it is Barth who has been disrespectful of God's sovereignty by denying that we cannot know the answer to a question which God has answered for us.

Barth's principal translator into English, Geoffrey Bromiley, commenting on this approach says that using "an admittedly biblical doctrine of divine freedom to contradict evident biblical data is an illustration of the arbitrary and illegitimate dogmatic thinking which elsewhere Barth rightly deplores."[21]

Our conclusion is that rejecting the doctrine of eternal punishment is equivalent to rejecting the clear teaching of the Bible. This can be done only by the wrong use of certain passages and the deliberate ignoring of other passages.

PART TWO

PRACTICAL ISSUES

CHAPTER TWELVE

WHY SHOULD WE TALK ABOUT JUDGMENT?

There is a medieval story of a man who in a dream saw a woman carrying a torch and a pitcher of water. The torch was to be used to burn the pleasures of heaven and the pitcher to quench the flames of hell. The story teaches that by eliminating the supposedly unworthy motives of desiring heaven and fearing hell, people could begin to love God for God's own sake.[1] Today, too, motivating people by referring to the future life is regarded as a lowly method, and consequently heaven and hell do not figure prominently in preaching.

WHY CHRIST SPOKE ON HELL

The simple fact that Christ spoke so often about hell should challenge Christians to reconsider their refusal to preach about it. In the Gospels the primary aim of Christ's words on hell was *not to inform people with details about what hell will be like*. In fact, though Christ taught that hell is an awful and eternal reality, he did not give a very clear picture about what hell is like.

A survey of Christ's teaching on the afterlife shows that his primary aim in teaching about hell was *to warn people* so that they would repent, live righteous lives and avert punishment. Jesus regarded preaching on hell as an appropriate way to motivate people. Peter Toon lists thirty-one different passages (not counting parallel passages) in the Gospels which contain warnings of hell.[2] We will examine a small sampling of these here.

The Evangelistic Situation (Mark 8:31-38)

While the word "hell" does not appear here in Christ's basic call to discipleship, future punishment is clearly implied. This is the discourse that begins with a call to take up the cross and follow Christ (v. 34). Christ goes on to argue for the worthwhileness of following him by appealing to the eternal consequences of the choices we make on earth. To attempt to "save" one's life by rejecting Christ is actually to "lose" it (v. 35). The word translated "lose" (*apollumi*) has the usual meaning of "destroy." It implies future punishment. This is clearer in the next verse: "What good is it for a man to gain the whole world, yet forfeit his soul? Or what can a man give in exchange for his soul?" (vv. 36, 37). Verse 38 says that when Christ returns in glory, he will be ashamed of those who are ashamed of him on earth.

Jesus is saying that the prospect of retribution makes following him worthwhile. This, then, is a use of the doctrine of hell in an evangelistic situation.

The Pastoral Situation (Mark 9:43-48)

Christ's warnings about hell are sometimes given in a pastoral situation. Once he said, "If your hand causes you to sin, cut it off. It is better for you to enter life maimed than with two hands to go into hell, where the fire never goes out." After making similar statements about the foot and the hand, he describes hell as a place where "their worm does not die, and the fire is not quenched" (Mark 9:43-48).

Today one of the biggest problems in the church is worldliness. People go through life with so much "excess baggage" that drags them down in their spiritual life. This passage is part of Christ's answer to this problem. The eye, the foot and the hand are not evil per se. But they can be used to lead a person away from God. In such cases, it would be better to be without them. Though we regard these as essential to life, they can be done away with because they are not indispensable from the perspective of eternity. The vision of heaven and hell gives us a proper perspective on earthly pursuits.

This passage teaches that when we are constructing our value system, we should take the eternal perspective of heaven and hell and make that a primary indicator for assessing how important a given thing is. If we do not avail ourselves of one of the Master's key strategies to attack worldliness, should we be surprised that today we have so little success in our attempts to attack it?

The Missionary Situation (Matt. 10:28)

The next example comes from a missionary situation when Christ instructed his disciples before they went out to preach (Matt. 10:5-42). He said, "Do not be afraid of those who kill the body but cannot kill the soul. Rather, be afraid of the one who can destroy both soul and body in hell" (10:28). The fear of the God who can cast us into hell was a motivation to persevere in witness amidst threats of trouble from powerful officials.

Around the time that I was studying this passage, I received word from Sri Lanka that the government was attempting to introduce legislation that would make our evangelistic work in villages illegal. My first response to this was fear. Then the truth of this passage came to me, bringing comfort and courage. I realized that we do not need to be afraid of these authorities. The only thing we should be afraid of is disobedience to the one who can cast us into hell. That helped me to be firm in the resolve to take the gospel to the unreached in villages of Sri Lanka, and to do so even if persecution and hardship were to come.

The above sampling shows that Jesus viewed the prospect of hell as a legitimate means of motivating people.

THE URGENCY OF REPENTANCE

If one of the reasons Jesus preached on hell was to urge people to repent and so avert the coming wrath, then universalism would result in a loss in the urgency of repentance. John Baillie recognized this in a book published in 1934 in which he predicted that the question of the fate of the unrepentant would be one of the growing-points of Christian thought. Baillie wrote, "If we decide for universalism, it must be for a form of it which does nothing to decrease the urgency of immediate repentance and which makes no promises to the procrastinating sinner." He went on to say that "it is doubtful whether such a form of the doctrine has yet been found."[3]

Fifty-six years after John Baillie penned these words, the trend he anticipated in the direction of universalism has taken place. But we can confidently say that no form of the doctrine has been found that captures the urgency of repentance which was seen in the preaching of Christ. Jesus' teaching method included warnings of the awesome prospect of eternal punishment. When we remove that, we remove from the gospel an effective, God-ordained means of leading people to repentance. We will end up with a weak gospel that cannot adequately combat sin and worldliness.

S. G. F. Brandon writes that since men gave up believing in hell, serious and widespread observable moral consequences have ensued in a way that demands "the attention of both theologian and sociologist."[4] A. W. Tozer says that "the vague and tenuous hope that God is too kind to punish the ungodly has become a deadly opiate to the consciences of millions." When they come under conviction and think that they should take the costly step of repentance, something inside them says, "Don't worry—it's not going to be that bad."

THE APPROPRIATENESS OF SPEAKING OF HELL TODAY

Many are reluctant to use the prospect of retribution in their preaching today because they feel it represents a base motivation unworthy of the gospel. As in the story of the torch and the pitcher, they like to encourage people to love God for God's own sake. But Christ would not have used this method if it wasn't a legitimate, loving and appropriate method to use.

To Inform People of the Facts

The most obvious reason for Christ's warnings about hell was he simply wanted to inform people of the facts. There is such a thing as punishment for wrong. If that is so, those who teach people about the way of life must include that in their teaching. The failure to do so would be strange, especially if it were a real possibility. And we know that it is.

The Natural Human Bent to Sinning

The natural human bent to sinning makes it appropriate to warn people about judgment. Because of our fallen state, we take to sin like a duck takes to water. Our normal choice is the way that leads to hell. Warning people of the consequences of sin could help them come to their senses and turn from this path that leads to destruction. God knew human nature well enough to know that warning is a necessary means to adopt in his dealings with humanity. So the Bible is replete with warnings of the consequences of sin.

Why then do we avoid this method today? One reason is that our generation has lost the biblical sense of the seriousness of sin. We do not recoil in horror over the fact that created human beings have rebelled against the Creator. The type of distress that Paul expressed at the start of Romans 9 over the lostness of the Jews would sound strange to most of us. He agreed that they were zealous, but he knew that their zeal was not based on knowledge (Rom. 10:2). So he said, "I have great sorrow and unceasing anguish in my heart." He was willing to be accursed and cut off from Christ for the sake of his brothers (Rom. 9:2, 3).

Many today feel that our generation is too sophisticated to endure talk of hell. So we preach mainly on what Christ will give people and how those are the things that they are looking for. But many self-sufficient people feel that they are not in need of anything from the church. They reject Christianity, saying it is for weak people, not for "self-made people" like themselves. They need to be confronted with the prospect of judgment. This is why, as I will argue later, judgment is a particularly relevant message to present to self-confident people who think they don't need the gospel.

But is it true that this generation is too sophisticated for a message of judgment? We know that this generation is as bad as, if not worse than, the earlier generations in the extent of its sinfulness.

Besides, our generation is not too sophisticated to heed warnings about the consequences of one's actions. We see this principle in operation all the time in daily life. Martin Marty reminds us that "anyone who brings up a child knows that rewards and punishments have to be a part of the value system and its enforcement." He says, "Rewards and punishments already exist on the sub-God secular level. There are report cards, demerits, merit badges, trophies, rewards, awards, detentions, expulsions, suspensions . . . and the like to ensure some framework, some structure for regulating and endorsing or disapproving action."[5] I fear that Christians have been so influenced by the mood of relativism that has invaded contemporary thinking about religion that we are afraid to make the type of assertions which are quite acceptable in other spheres of life.

Perhaps our reluctance to preach on hell is because we ourselves find it hard to accept that a person's sinfulness is serious enough to merit so severe a punishment as hell. If so, we need to go back to the Scriptures and get a fresh sense of the seriousness of sin. This would help us overcome the influence of the message we hear daily from society that man is not so bad after all.

Indeed, preaching on hell is unpalatable to our generation. And that is because ours is a sinful generation. Part of the preacher's calling is to challenge man's commitment to sinfulness. People will not like to hear that. But some will be rebuked by it and will repent and be saved.

Unrighteousness Seems to Be More Rewarding

Preaching on judgment is also needed today because in this fallen world unrighteousness often seems to be more rewarding than the way of obedience. This is a false perception, for the pleasures of sin are fleeting (Heb. 11:25). But it is a powerful source of temptation to most people.

Jesus addresses this temptation when he asks us to store up for ourselves treasures in heaven (Matt. 6:19-21). The way of disobedience may bring for us more treasures on earth than we would find through the way of obedience. There is a great lure to wealth (see Matt. 13:22; 1 Tim. 6:10). In the face of such a powerful source of temptation to disobedience, people need to be confronted with a more powerful source of encouragement to obedience. Jesus knew that the prospect of eternal reward was such a source. So he told people to lay up or invest their treasures in heaven.

Jesus used this method when he told the story of the rich farmer (Luke 12:16-21). The farmer was a person who would be regarded by earthly standards as a great success in life. But God calls him a "fool" because he was "not rich toward God." He had stored sufficient to ensure a comfortable retirement, but he had no resources stored up for the next life.

Recently many people in Sri Lanka invested their savings in some finance companies that promised a very high interest. But these companies crashed suddenly, and many lost their life savings. Though they offered a high interest, they were not secure. A prudent market analyst would advise us to invest our money in a place that is both secure and also promised a good yield. The "bank of heaven" is such a place.

Paul also mentions the laying up of another type of treasure in Romans 2:5: "Because of your stubbornness and your unrepentant heart, you are storing up wrath against yourself for the day of God's wrath." The word translated "storing up" is the same word (thēsaurizō) that Jesus used in the passage we just cited. It means to "lay up as treasure." So the Bible presents the choice facing people very vividly. They can either store up the treasure of eternal blessing or of eternal wrath.

When we appeal to people to accept heaven rather than hell, we are giving advice similar to that of a prudent market analyst. We tell them that though the way of sin may bring an immediate yield in terms of temporary pleasure, when God's wrath becomes operative, that structure will crash. On that day those who invested in the Kingdom of Heaven will find that their investment will yield an unimaginably great return. We are appealing to their common sense.

Paul expresses his belief in the motivational value of the prospect of the afterlife in overcoming the lure of sinful pleasure in 1 Corinthians 15:32-34:

> If the dead are not raised, "Let us eat and drink, for tomorrow we die." Do not be misled: "Bad company corrupts good character." Come back to your senses as you ought,

and stop sinning; for there are some who are ignorant of God—I say this to your shame.

We agree that loving God for his own sake is a noble motivation, possibly even the noblest motivation, for Christian discipleship. But it is not the only motivation. Given our fallen state, we are often unable to think such noble thoughts. God, who knows us better than anyone else, knew that in order to draw us to himself he needed to use a method that would somehow get through to our sin-warped minds. So he warns us of the prospect of retribution.

JUDGMENT AND THE PLURALISTIC MOOD

A major reason why contemporary Christians do not like to speak about hell is that pluralism and relativism, especially regarding religious matters, has become an important philosophy in contemporary society. The trend because of this is to unite, to accept those of different traditions and try to understand them and live in harmony with them. The doctrine of hell does not unite people according to this pluralistic ideal. It speaks of the peak of separation—an eternal separation of the saved and the lost. The division of humanity into the saved and the lost is an offense to many modern forms of pluralism. Because of this pluralistic mood, hell has become culturally inaccessible to most people today.

The mood of relativism has influenced the evangelical movement too. Evangelicals are often apologetic about the biblical view of retribution. They say that they wish that what the Bible says about the punishment of sinners is not true, that they find it hard to accept this doctrine emotionally, but that because the Bible teaches it they are forced to believe it.

This type of thinking is understandable, given our human frailty and inability to fully understand God's ways. We do not see the seriousness of sin as strongly as God sees it. But many today seem to be proud that their hearts rebel against the judgment of

God. The message they convey to an outsider is that they think God is wrong and unfair, but that's what he is going to do, so they reluctantly include it in their statement of faith.

Such thinking is alien to the attitude of the biblical apologist. Jude describes apologetics as "contend[ing] for the faith that was once for all entrusted to the saints" (Jude 3). Peter describes it as "always be[ing] prepared to give an answer to everyone who asks you to give the reason for the hope that you have" (1 Pet. 3:15). The word translated "an answer" here, *apologian*, comes from the courtroom, where it is used for giving a formal defense against specific charges (see Acts 22:1; 25:16; 2 Tim. 4:16 for this use).

So the apologist's call is to demonstrate the justice of God's ways, in response to the objections brought by others. Many Christians today are apologizing for God rather than contending for his truth. Their hearers may praise them for their broadmindedness and say that they are not like other evangelicals. But they remain critical of God. This is like a lawyer who saves his reputation at the cost of having his client convicted!

If we apologize for a doctrine that we hold, it should not surprise us when many of our hearers reject or ignore that doctrine. We believe that the apologizing attitude towards hell of many evangelicals has unwittingly contributed to the growth of universalism today.

SHOULD WE FRIGHTEN PEOPLE INTO THE KINGDOM?

Many people say they do not preach about hell because it is not correct to frighten people into the Kingdom. Those who present this objection cite examples of irresponsible preaching about hell when people were threatened or emotionally manipulated in a way that was an insult to their God-given personhood.

But the misuse of the topic of hell does not warrant its disuse. It challenges us to explore proper ways of warning people about hell (on this, see Chapters 14 and 15). Even Christ saw fear as a legitimate way to challenge people. He specifically referred to fear when he asked his disciples to "be afraid of the one who can destroy both soul and body in hell" (Matt. 10:28).

Now, our goal in preaching about hell is not to frighten people. It is to deliver them from hell so they can be recipients of God's salvation. Any sane society appreciates the urgent need to warn people about imminent danger. Governments spend much money on setting up sophisticated meteorological equipment and placing qualified personnel in charge of them so they can warn people to be prepared if a dangerous storm is on the way. Warning people about judgment is something like this.

If a doctor fails to warn his patient of a growing cancer, and the patient dies due to the lack of appropriate treatment, the doctor is likely to be held responsible. If this principle were adopted when considering the preacher's need to warn people of impending judgment, which is much more serious than cancer, how many preachers will be guilty today! It is sobering to note that the Bible *does* speak of such guilt:

> When I say to a wicked man, "You will surely die," and you do not warn him or speak out to dissuade him from his evil ways in order to save his life, that wicked man will die for his sin, and I will hold you accountable for his blood. But if you warn the wicked man and he does not turn from his wickedness or from his evil ways, he will die for his sin; but you will have saved yourself. (Ezek. 3:18, 19)

If a doctor used fear to persuade some who were resisting his advice to break a potentially dangerous habit, and by doing so saved them from sure death, few would find fault with him. But that is not the way many people respond to preaching about hell. This is because there is a difference between changing one's habits to avoid an illness and repenting of one's whole way of life to avoid a judgment that is to take place, if at all, in the "distant future." People don't mind a temporary change to save their skin. But they are not eager to repent of their independence from God. That involves giving up things they enjoy. Satan will use this distaste for repentance to keep them blinded and resistant to repentance (2 Cor. 4:4).

Besides, even though we may tolerate fear over an emergency like cancer, ours is a generation that is afraid of fear. We are so dedicated to the task of feeling good that rightness is often associated with a nice feeling. And fear is not a nice feeling. Preachers too have been influenced by this mood.

We should fear fear if we have no solution to offer to those whom we warn. But we have a solution. The warning of judgment is but a prelude to the announcement of the message of God's grace freely offered to humanity. The main thrust of any evangelistic message is not hell but salvation. So technically when we are preaching about hell, we are not frightening people into heaven. We may frighten people away from hell so they can joyously accept God's gift of heaven.

The preaching of hell alerts the unbeliever to his or her need for salvation, and fear may have some part in bringing one to realize this need. The preaching of grace provides the path to receiving this salvation.

While technologically developed nations may try to suppress the feeling of fear, fear is perhaps the dominant emotion that influences the life of people in many other societies. So when we preach on judgment in such societies we are dealing with a felt and acknowledged need.

In the technologically advanced West this emotion of fear may be denied, but it is a reality which may have been numbed in some form. This is the "aspirin" generation which is used to eliminating discomfort through symptomatic relief. But such elimination of discomfort can be very dangerous if it keeps us from looking for the cause of the discomfort. Just as pain is a friend which can direct us to a serious problem in our body, fear can be a friend that alerts us to our need for salvation from hell.

AN ANALOGY

Let me explain the appropriateness of using fear in preaching by using an analogy from day-to-day life. People today are constantly faced with the temptation of illicit sexual enjoyment. Sometimes they succumb to temptation and act in ways that are repulsive to their own personal tastes and values. When tempted thus, the fear of getting caught may be what finally keeps a person from sinning.

When a young Christian passes an establishment that shows pornographic films, something within him says, "Why don't you go in and see what it's like?" He is strongly tempted to yield to that suggestion. Suddenly the thought comes to him, "What if this place is raided and I get caught? What will that do to my testimony as a Christian?" The fear of getting caught helps him to resist the temptation to go in.

Ideally he should have resisted this temptation through his love for God and his desire to please him. But in his weakened state these noble motivations had no affect on him. What got him was the fear of getting caught.

Observing his life after he avoided the temptation, one would not say that he is a psychologically unhealthy person motivated by the tyranny of guilt. He would invariably be happy that he was saved just in time from doing something foolish and harmful. His life is not controlled by a morbid fear of sin. That has now been forgotten, and he is free to joyously experience the blessings of grace. The fear of getting caught was simply a tool that God used at a crisis time to rescue him from a terrible calamity.

It is like that with our proclamation of judgment. The proclamation of judgment arrests people so that they will be open to hearing the message of grace. Because they are blinded by Satan from seeing the glory of the gospel, they may not find grace attractive. They may open their minds to considering another way only after they are shocked into realizing the awful consequences of sin.

Once the message of grace takes root in the heart, the message of judgment pales into insignificance. Later when someone asks, "Why do you serve God?" they would not say, "So I can avert judgment." Rather they would say something like, "Because I love him," or "Because this is the best way there is to live."

A PIE-IN-THE-SKY RELIGION?

Our emphasis on the prospect of future reward and punishment influencing life on earth may remind some readers of the "pie in the sky in the world by and by" theology. This theology promised people, like Christian slaves, a heavenly reward and thus encouraged them passively to endure oppression and hardship without doing much to change their situation. Such passivity in the face of injustice is dishonoring to God, who is portrayed in the Bible as abhorring injustice.

Indeed the Christian believes that it profits a person nothing to gain the whole world while losing his own soul (Mark 8:36). But that refers to gaining the whole world at the cost of one's soul. It does not mean that having ambitions on earthly matters is wrong. It means that our earthly ambitions spring out of our commitment to our heavenly Lord, who is also the Lord of all the earth.

The Christian approach to the world is one of service springing from the heavenly perspective. We are willing to endure hardship for the sake of our principles, knowing that in the end it will be worthwhile because the final verdict and reward for our efforts will be given at the judgment. This tells us that the principles and practices which contribute to God's eternal plan, and not temporary pleasure or wealth, are what are most important in life. So we will not compromise Kingdom values for success on earth.

The prospect of a future judgment, therefore, is something that motivates us to action and not something that acts as an opiate which soothes oppressed people and keeps them from striving for their legitimate aspirations. Karl Marx saw a form of Christianity that gave room for this to happen and leveled a charge against the church which it deserved. But what he saw was not biblical Christianity.

Paul was a person who exemplified the biblical commitment to eternal principles and still expressed concern for temporal rights. He urged Christians to set their hearts on things above (Col. 3:1). He asked them to be willing to endure hardship and warned that all who seek to live a godly life in Christ Jesus will be persecuted (2 Tim. 2:3; 3:12). He himself sang praises to God after he had been unjustly beaten and put into prison in Philippi. But when the Philippian officials came to release him, he protested about the way his rights as a Roman citizen had been violated (Acts 16:22-40). After he was arrested in Jerusalem, he used some very well thought out methods in his defense (Acts 21:37–26:32).

Injustice dishonors God. The Christian battles all that dishonors God, even when the victim of the injustice is himself. But in this battle he uses only those means which will honor God. So if justice can be secured only by methods which contradict God's ways, such as the use of violence, he would rather endure hardship than compromise his Christian principles. Here the heavenly perspective helps him endure, because he regards eternal principles to be of greater value than temporal gain secured by the wrong means.

CHAPTER THIRTEEN

LOSTNESS AS A MOTIVATION TO EVANGELISM

It is often said that universalism cuts the nerve of evangelism. But some universalists disagree. In this chapter we will show that belief in eternal punishment is linked to evangelism in the Scriptures.

THE PRIORITY OF REACHING THE UNREACHED

Recently there has been a lot of unfortunate conflict in the church over the relationship between social concern and evangelism. It must grieve the heart of God when Christians pit evangelism against social concern. Our responsibility is to obey God's call to be a servant community in this needy world. This involves both social concern and evangelism. Sometimes Christians want to be able to put things in neat little packages so that they have a simple system for determining which activity has priority. Perhaps this is a sign of a western malady. Christian service does not always come in such simple packages. Each situation demands sensitivity and creativity in deciding how we should respond.

Yet trying to do both evangelism and social action is not easy. In our Youth for Christ ministry we have tried to do both and have found it difficult to keep the proper balance between these two aspects. It is much easier to concentrate on one and neglect the other, which is what many do.

When we start meeting the social needs of people, we soon discover that there are so many needs that cry out for our attention. If we did only social work, and did so with extraordinary commitment, we would still have many needs that we could not get to. We would be so busy that it would be difficult to have time for evangelistic programs.

With so much to do, where would there be the time or the energy to get involved in reaching those out of contact with us who have not heard of Christ? We would give ourselves to such a ministry only if we knew that it was utterly urgent. If we knew that everyone was going to be saved in the end, then the urgency of reaching these unreached people would be reduced considerably. Given our already crowded program, we would let this work slip from the place of supreme priority on our agenda.

That this has indeed happened has been the observation of many. N. T. Wright, in a preparatory paper leading to the Nairobi General Assembly of the World Council of Churches, wrote the following:

> That the universalist, believing that God will save all men anyway, has therefore the leisure to get on exclusively with other matters is seen clearly in much modern thought, which has abandoned serious evangelism in favour of some form of social action—particularly but sadly in the World Council of Churches, where "salvation" has been given such a firm this-worldly orientation that evangelism often becomes simply irrelevant.[1]

A SPUR TO EVANGELISM

While universalism can act as a deterrent to biblical evangelism, a biblically informed understanding of lostness and anticipation of judgment can be a significant source of motivation to it.

It was lostness that lay behind Paul's "heart's desire and prayer to God for the Israelites . . . that they may be saved" (Rom. 10:1). That desire arose from the fact that "they did not know the righteousness that comes from God" (see vv. 2-4). Their lostness was a source of "great sorrow and unceasing anguish in [his] heart" (Rom. 9:2).

If we love people, our hearts will be broken over their lostness. This will produce in us a passion like that of Paul when he cried, "I could wish that I myself were cursed and cut off from Christ for the sake of my brothers, those of my own race" (Rom. 9:3). Such a vision of lostness motivated Paul to do the great work that he did for the Kingdom.

We are often reluctant to get down to witnessing for Christ because of spiritual lethargy. The prospect that the person before us might go to hell could help overcome this lethargy. It gives a sense of urgency to the task. Jude, urging Christians to evangelism among those who have been misled by false teachers, says, "Snatch others from the fire [of judgment] and save them" (v. 23).

Some object that this is not a noble motive for service. Maybe. But at least it helps save a dying person. We would not expect a life-saver to hesitate to rescue a drowning person because he was not sure whether his motives in doing so were correct. He would jump into the water as soon as possible to save the person before it was too late.

Others would object that it is unhealthy for a Christian to have bondage to duty as a driving force. We agree. But what we are presenting here is not bondage to duty in a psychologically unhealthy manner. It is the commitment to duty by one who delights to show love to others but who knows that sometimes "the flesh" prompts him in the direction of lethargy. At such times "the passion for souls" overcomes the lethargy. Once the action is complete, we are so happy that we have done it.

When I am confronted with a potential witnessing situation I usually think of numerous excuses to keep me from talking about Christ. Most often it is the sense of duty that finally drives me to witness. But I have never regretted doing it. In fact this activity, commenced out of a sense of duty, often turns out to be a thrilling experience.

Problems, however, may arise when people are forced to conform to an inflexible program of witnessing. Sometimes Christians are forced to come up with certain measurable results in terms of "decisions for Christ" or "persons witnessed to." Sometimes they are forced to talk to people when they are tired and need a rest or when they should be doing something else like playing or enjoying their family. These are misuses of the principle of commitment to duty.

There are some people, such as those suffering from pathological guilt or other complexes, who are unable to respond to calls to duty in a healthy fashion because of psychological scars in their lives. These are exceptions to the rule. Pastoral concerns would cause one to modify the usual method when working with such people. But we must never make exceptions to the rule.

The vision of lostness was a strong motivating force in the lives of some of the heroes of Christian history. The seventeenth-century Scottish preacher Samuel Rutherford once told a person, "I would lay my dearest joys in the gap between you and eternal destruction."[2] Hudson Taylor said, "I would have never thought of going to China had I not believed that the Chinese were lost and needed Christ." D. L. Moody told an audience in London, "If I believed there was no hell, I am sure I would be off tomorrow for America." He said he would give up going from town to town and spending day and night "urging men to escape the damnation of hell."[3] William Booth said he would wish that his Salvation Army workers could spend "one night in hell" in order to see the urgency of their evangelistic task.

My wife has found the doctrine of hell to be a key ingredient in her value system. She has a price to pay because of my travels here and there preaching the gospel. Combining her own ministry with being a mother has also not been easy. Many people today measure success and fulfillment entirely by this-worldly criteria. When influenced by such people, questions come to her mind as to whether the price paid to live for reaching the lost is worth paying.

At one of those times she read a sermon on hell by an American pastor, the Rev. Bill Hybels. It reminded her of the urgency of saving people from eternal damnation.[4] Into her heart came the conviction that her lot was one of great privilege, not deprivation. There was only sorrow that she was not doing enough. She regularly urges me to speak to my relatives about their eternal salvation, a thing I am often reluctant to do.

MOTIVATION THROUGH CULTURAL IMPERIALISM

When I was a theological student in America in the early seventies, I participated in many missions conferences. These enriching experiences helped me to sense the message of missions that burns through the Bible. But sometimes there would emerge a theme which troubled me greatly. Examples of the so-called depravity of the peoples on the mission fields were presented in an attempt to motivate Christians to give to missions. But this was done in a way that indicated that those on the so-called mission fields were culturally inferior to those in "Christian" countries. I recognized this as an instance of cultural imperialism. Sadly, the history of missions records that there have been prominent Christians who used nationalism and its related cultural imperialism or arrogance to motivate Christians to missionary involvement.[5]

During the past few decades we have seen the myth of western superiority demolished in the minds of many sensitive westerners. Numerous factors contributed to this, such as the disruption of the great western empires, the rise of powerful non-western political and economic forces, the new appreciation for the great cultural heritages of Third World countries, and the rise of Third World leaders in many fields who are admired in the West.

Many sensitive Christians in the West, embarrassed by the regrettable past of cultural arrogance, seem to have shied away from all approaches to missions that suggest that Christians are in any way better than others. Christians in the former colonies of western powers have had to face even greater embarrassment over their past ties with the "Christian" rulers who were guilty of extreme cultural imperialism. So there is a hesitancy among Christians worldwide to assert that one group is in any way superior to another.

The doctrine of the lostness of humanity apart from Christ seems to imply that Christians are superior to others. But an understanding of the biblical teaching about grace shows that Christians could never consider themselves superior to anyone else because they did nothing to merit their salvation. There is therefore a big difference between the doctrine of lostness and the myth of cultural imperialism. Their association in missionary motivation in the past was wrong, and so is the modern practice of jettisoning them together.

All cultures have been tainted by sin. But some of the areas identified in earlier days as being culturally depraved did not have to do with sin at all. I would, for example, never succumb to any pressure to stop eating my meals using my fingers. I use what to me is a somewhat unnatural, unenjoyable and inefficient method of eating with the fork and knife when I am in the West out of consideration for the sensitivities of my western friends. But I gladly revert to the method I am used to as soon as possible. There have been times when Christians were challenged to be involved in missions so they could help free people of, among other things, "savage" practices like eating with their fingers. The cry was to Christianize the world, but Christianizing was often confused with Westernizing.

What we need is to focus again on the lostness of humanity. People are alienated from God and are headed for judgment in all cultures. They need to be saved whether they come from so-called Christian countries or non-Christian countries, whether they are members of churches or not.

PREACHING ON LOSTNESS

One way to focus on lostness is to preach about it. Paul urged the Ephesians to remember what they were before their conversion. This passage is so vivid and so alien to the modern Christian pulpit that I will quote from it now:

> Therefore, remember that you who are formerly Gentiles by birth and called "uncircumcised" by those who call themselves "the circumcision" . . . remember that at that time you were separate from Christ, excluded from citizenship in Israel and foreigners to the covenants of the promise, without hope and without God in the world. But now in Christ Jesus you who once were far away have been brought near through the blood of Christ. (Eph 2:11-13)

Expounding passages like this will help Christians appreciate their salvation more and also motivate them to take the message of this salvation to those who are lost.

ONE OF MANY SOURCES OF MOTIVATION

Lostness is not the only source of motivation to evangelism. The Scriptures give many more, such as the pressure exerted by Christ's love in us (2 Cor. 5:14), the love we have for Christ (John 14:15), our conviction about the efficacy of Christ's work (2 Cor. 5:14b), the prospect of being rewarded for our services (2 Cor. 5:9, 10), the fear associated with standing before God at the judgment (2 Cor. 5:11, Matt. 10:27, 28), the thrill of being ambassadors of Christ (2 Cor. 5:20), and the desire to glorify God (1 Cor. 10:31).

At different times different sources of motivation will exert more influence upon us. For example, when authorities persecute us and try to stop us from evangelizing, Jesus urges us to be motivated by the fear of God the Judge, who can destroy the soul and body in hell. This fear will help us overcome the fear of earthly authorities who can kill the body but not the soul (Matt. 10:17-28).

People have debated the issue of which is the highest of these motivations. I believe that is an unnecessary debate. We should make sure that each element of the biblical picture of motivation is presented in our ministries as part of our effort to proclaim the "whole counsel of God." Then we would have in our minds the raw material which God uses to help us live as he would have us live.

CHAPTER FOURTEEN

PROCLAIMING THE MESSAGE OF JUDGMENT

M any people shy away from talking and preaching about judgment because they don't know how to do it. Fortunately the Bible has given us numerous examples for our instruction. We will now look at some of these, especially from the ministry of Jeremiah.

USE CAREFUL REASONING

Reasoning is a very important aspect of all preaching and witness, as the book of Acts shows.[1] We must present the case for the truth so that our hearers may be persuaded of its truthfulness and value. Reasoning is a method we use in preaching about judgment too.

When Paul spoke privately to the Roman governor Felix and his wife he "discoursed on righteousness, self-control and the judgment" (Acts 24:25). The word translated "discoursed" (*dialegomai*) has the idea of "discussed" or "dialogued." What took place was a discussion on religion in which Paul presented his case for the Christian understanding of judgment.

The most important key to reasoning on behalf of judgment

is to tell people why judgment is coming. This is well expressed in Jeremiah 16:10-13. God anticipates that people will ask why judgment is to come. So he instructs Jeremiah, "When you tell these people all this and they ask you, 'Why has he Lord decreed such a great disaster against us? What wrong have we done? What sin have we committed against the Lord our God?' then say to them, 'It is because your fathers forsook me. . . . But you have behaved more wickedly than your fathers'" (vv. 10-12a). Jeremiah is to tell them the reason for the judgment, which is disobedience. Then he must describe the punishment that disobedience reaps: "So I will throw you out of this land into a land neither you nor your fathers have known . . ." (v. 13).

When we reason with people, we resurface a sense that the sin in every person must be punished. There is an innate sense in every human being that wrongdoing must be punished. People, however, suppress this and go on sinning. Paul says of sinful humanity that "although *they know* God's righteous decree that *those who do such things deserve death*, they not only continue to do these very things but also approve of those who practice them" (Rom. 1:32).

A successful American entertainer was interviewed on television shortly before his death. He knew that he was going to die very soon. The interviewer asked him what he feared most. His answer was, "That there is a hell." As he faced death he admitted to a fear of judgment that one would not have expected by observing his carefree and godless life.

Despite this innate sense of justice, hell is culturally distant to most people today. Many have hardly ever heard the idea mentioned. So it does not generally come into their thinking. Charles Spurgeon said, over a hundred years ago, that "it is shocking to reflect that a change in the weather has more effect on some men's lives than the dread alternative of heaven or hell."[2] Today if hell is mentioned at all it is usually as a slang expression. In such an environment simply proclaiming hell may not be an adequate strategy of communication. There are some people to whom hell was a strange concept but who have come to trust in Christ after a simple proclamation of judgment. But those are exceptions to the rule.

By reasoning about the reality of retribution, we seek to resurrect that buried sense of judgment that is in all people. Through reasoning the mind sees the logic behind what we say. It resonates with the buried sense of judgment. In this way, the Holy Spirit uses our reasoning as the means by which he exercises his ministry of convincing the world of judgment (John 16:8).

I have a friend, Al Nix, who is a Youth for Christ worker in the New York area. He came from a poor family, but he did very well in school and secured a place at the prestigious Princeton University. He was greatly admired in his neighborhood and was presented as an example of what a black student from a poor neighborhood could achieve in life. But deep inside there was a restlessness in him. He knew he was missing the most important things in life.

One day he read some Christian tracts and, in his words, "got scared out of [his] socks." Even though he did not come from a religious family, he felt convicted of sin. That buried sense that sin must be judged surfaced and triggered off a process that finally resulted in his becoming a Christian.

Today Al is back in his hometown seeking to reach the youth there with the gospel of Christ. Recently he spoke on judgment at a meeting where the majority of the audience was not Christian. He told them that when they do something wrong at home, something tells them they are in trouble if their action is discovered. When they do badly at an exam, they know they will get a bad grade. After giving many earthly examples of the principle that we reap what we sow, he said that all this points to the most important judgment that is to come. At the end of the meeting a youth who seemed to care nothing about God or his ways said he wanted to talk to Al because he was convicted by the message.

While I was writing this book, I talked to many Christians about the topic of hell. I was surprised to find that the fear of hell had had a big part to play in leading a significant number of them to the point of commitment to Christ. Some of these people came from sophisticated backgrounds and were highly educated. But they were not too sophisticated to realize that sin had to be punished.

A lot of the preaching and talking about hell that has taken place in recent years has been lacking in this aspect of reasoning. It has been descriptive, and, as we shall see, there is a place for that. Some of it has taken the form of warning. And there is a place for that too. But there has been little reasoning.

There is a challenge here to the intellectuals in the church. They must seek to argue for this doctrine in an intellectually persuasive form. It is significant that some of the most stimulating thinking on the doctrine of hell to appear (or re-appear) in recent times has come from three of the great intellectual giants of the western church: Jonathan Edwards and Charles Finney of America and C. S. Lewis of England.[3]

DESCRIBE THE SIN THAT MERITS JUDGMENT

The text we looked at earlier from Jeremiah (16:10-13) shows that we are not simply to stop with the statement that the people are sinners and so are headed for judgment. That is too general. General statements are too vague to grab the attention of people, especially if the message is an unpleasant one. After listening to such a message the hearers could say that it does not apply to them. God asks Jeremiah to describe what the sins of the people are: "See how each of you is following the stubbornness of his evil heart instead of obeying me" (v. 12b).

The example given above describes the basic cause for judgment—rebellion against God. As we showed earlier, the basic cause for judgment is unbelief or the refusal to live under God and his ways. The Bible teaches that this basic sin (unbelief) expresses itself in more overt acts of disobedience to God's ways. This is explained by Paul in Romans 1:18-32. Here he first describes man's basic decision to be independent of God (vv. 18-23) and then shows how this decision results in numerous other sins (vv. 24-32).

When we proclaim judgment we need to point out the sin of rebellion against God. In the passage under consideration this is described quite plainly: "Each of you is following the stubbornness of his evil heart instead of obeying me" (Jer. 16:12). In the book of Jeremiah and in the other prophets this basic sin is also described more vividly by the use of various analogies. Jeremiah 2:20-22 is a good example:

> *Refusing to be servants of God:* "Long ago you broke off your yoke and tore off your bonds; you said, 'I will not serve you!'"

> *Spiritual prostitution:* "Indeed, on every high hill and under every spreading tree you lay down as a prostitute."

> *Corruption of a vine of pure stock:* "I had planted you like a choice vine of sound and reliable stock. How then did you turn against me into a corrupt, wild vine?"

> *Unclean:* "Although you wash yourself with soda and use an abundance of soap, the stain of your guilt is still before me."

Four different analogies describe the basic sin of independence from God.

Yet, despite the use of vivid analogies, our hearers may find that to be a vague charge. Thus it is necessary to describe specific sins committed by our hearers as evidence of rebellion against God. This was what Paul did in Romans 1. Jeremiah did this in his preaching too. His book has different passages condemning the false prophets, the kings, the priests, the people and the neighboring nations. Specific sins are described relating to the different groups.

In chapter 7, Jeremiah addresses the people of Judah and gives a most interesting list of sins that the people are guilty of. *Religious infidelity*, which is the basic sin, appears here also. The people are guilty of following other gods (v. 6), trusting in the deceptive words of the false prophets (v. 8), standing before God in the temple after following other gods (vv. 9, 10), and burning incense to Baal (v. 9). Contemporary examples of this category today would include following any religion that does not acknowledge Christ as Lord and resorting to demonic practices like witchcraft and spiritism.

In true prophetic tradition *social injustice* appears in Jeremiah's list of sins. The people are asked to act justly and to abstain from oppressing the alien, the fatherless and the widow (vv. 5, 6). It is sad to note that many today who claim to be biblical abstain from condemning such sins in their evangelistic preaching.

Jeremiah also mentions *violence*, and the particular sin he renounces is the shedding of innocent blood (v. 6). Then there are sins like *stealing, murder, perjury* and *sexual immorality* (v. 9), all of which are extremely relevant to the situation today.

A look at the history of the church will show us that where preaching has been effective, it has included listings of specific sins of the people that need to be repented of and forsaken. Revival has always been accompanied by the fearless denunciation of sin and the clear presentation of the coming judgment.[4]

Preaching must not only be theologically orthodox. It must be relevant. A key to relevance is specificity. So long as we keep our hearers away from the specific ways in which truth is applied, the sermon will be too weak to be a catalyst for change in their lives. They could dismiss it as not applying personally to them.

Being specific does not mean that each sermon on judgment must contain a comprehensive catalog of sins. The passage we examined above from Jeremiah 7 was somewhat general and comprehensive, as it was given to the whole people of Judah. But at other times we see Jeremiah's specificity expressed in terms of distinct messages to different groups of people. The false prophets are to be punished for lying and deceiving the people with their messages of peace (5:31; 8:10-12; 14:13-16; 29:31, 32). The corrupt will be judged for their dishonesty (5:26-29). Chapter 22 is an announcement of judgment against the kings, which includes a listing of their sins.

Sometimes in our talk we may be specific but cover a cross section of people, describing specific sins of each group of people. Jeremiah 2:8 is a good example of this: "The priests did not ask, 'Where is the Lord?' Those who deal with the law did not know me; the leaders rebelled against me. The prophets prophesied by Baal, following worthless idols." Specific sins of four groups of people are listed in this one verse.

While specificity makes a message more relevant, it does not necessarily make it popular. Often people prefer to have sermons remaining at the level of general principles. Such sermons are commended for their orthodoxy, even though they may have not had much of a penetrative impact upon the hearers. When the preacher gets specific, people get uneasy. To overcome this uneasiness they often find fault with the preacher and his sermon.

SPEAK ABOUT JUDGMENT TO ALL TYPES OF PEOPLE

Some claim that though hell may be an appropriate topic among simple-minded folk, it is not appropriate among intellectually sophisticated people. The section above on reasoning the doctrine showed that this is not true.

We see that Jeremiah addressed all classes of people with his message of judgment. He was most harsh on the religious leaders, the priests and false prophets, who led others astray.[5] Those who follow the teachings of the false prophets will also be judged (14:16). Jeremiah denounced kings and rulers (22:1-30) and suffered for it. Once he had the scroll containing his messages burned by King Jehoiakim (chap. 36). There are few things that writers, preachers, and other communicators of truth dread as much as losing their notes!

Sometimes Jeremiah predicted that the whole nation would be judged. King Zedekiah's officials put him in prison because his message against the nation seemed treacherous and unpatriotic (chap. 37). Jeremiah even talked about the most revered national institution, the temple of Jerusalem, when he denounced the people. He said, "Do not trust in deceptive words and say, 'This is the temple of the Lord, the temple of the Lord, the temple of the Lord!'" (7:4). Jeremiah did not subscribe to the motto, "My country, right or wrong."

Paul also spoke to all types of people about judgment. When he addressed the sophisticated intellectuals of Athens, he included judgment in his message (Acts 17:31), even though "Greek thought had no room for such an eschatological judgment as the biblical revelation announces."[6] Of course, Paul's speech in Athens was a philosophically oriented discourse. Paul also talked about judgment with the Roman governor Felix and his wife (Acts 24:25).

Some think that speaking of judgment is appropriate only among people recognized by society as "big sinners," like prostitutes, drug addicts and robbers. Indeed, such people need to hear about judgment. But usually they are so discouraged by the hopelessness of their situation that they accept the idea of judgment without much hesitancy. What they need to hear most is that God can rescue them out of their hopeless state. They need to be told of the love and redeeming power of God.

Those who live in arrogant, self-sufficient independence from God are the ones who most need to hear about judgment. Preaching about God's love may leave them unimpressed. They would say that such a message is good for weak people, who need the "crutch" of religion to help them face the challenges of life, but not for them.

Once, after I had spoken about the love of God using the parable of the prodigal son, a successful businessman who was there spoke to me. He made it known to me that he did not need the type of religion I had commended. Weak people needed that, but he had reached the top without God. I went home troubled and wondered what features of the gospel would impress people like him.

I concluded that while the message of love is always relevant, I must also present the sovereignty and holiness of the Judge of all the earth to self-sufficient people like the one I met at that meeting. That would help jolt them out of their careless indifference to God's grace. After all, it was at the self-sufficient Pharisees that Jesus' harshest words of judgment were directed. Some who are at first unimpressed by the gentleness of God may come to respect the strength of God. That respect could be the stepping-stone that leads to their listening to the rest of the gospel.

This is the way God dealt with the "contented and prosperous" Nebuchadnezzar (Dan. 4:4). God told him, "The decision is announced by messengers; the holy ones declare the verdict, so that the living may know that the Most High is sovereign over the kingdoms of men and gives them to anyone he wishes and sets them over the lowliest of men" (Dan. 4:17). This began a process that ended in the conversion of Nebuchadnezzar into a worshiper of Yahweh.

Nebuchadnezzar had seen many evidences of God's power and love before. All of them had impressed him. But soon after these experiences he returned to his attitude of arrogant indifference toward God. The vision of God's sovereignty and then the ensuing judgment upon Nebuchadnezzar finally resulted in his conversion.

Self-sufficient people often become receptive to any religious thinking only when they come to accept their own finiteness, which is a fact they had tried to deny. Often they come to this point only after a humiliation or a fall. But even at this point, while the love of God will certainly be a great comfort, often it is the holiness and sovereignty of God that impresses most. This was so with Nebuchadnezzar.

I have a friend who rejected his Christian convictions in young adulthood and became consumed in a quest for material success. In a short time he climbed to the top of the social ladder. He had an arrogant disdain for the things of God. Suddenly he encountered serious financial setbacks. In desperation he resorted to illegal methods of making money. He ended up in jail. His wife left him. Everything seemed to have gone wrong. In jail he decided to commit suicide by hanging. The attempt, however, was a failure as his feet got caught in the bars of a window.

He had to remain in this hanging position for some time. While he was there he had a vision of God. What he saw was not a kind and gentle Father but a strong and awesome holy Judge. This vision led him finally to the point of repentance and commitment to God.

In the so-called Third World, the preaching of judgment affirms an acknowledged emotion—the emotion of fear. While those in the West may try to deny it, the people in many technologically less-developed societies live with it daily and have elaborate religious ceremonies to try and avert the dangers they fear. When we speak of judgment to them, that inner sense of the inevitability of retribution resounds very readily in their minds. We have addressed a felt need. The door is open to provide the eternal solution to their fears: liberation in Christ Jesus.

PRESENT JUDGMENT AS PART OF THE CASE FOR RIGHTEOUSNESS

In Chapter 12 we pointed out that one of the primary things Christ hoped to achieve by preaching on judgment was motivating people to repent and to follow the path of righteousness. As this topic has already been dealt with in some depth, here we will only give some examples of Old Testament preaching that uses this argument.

Jeremiah spoke about judgment with the hope that his hearers would repent. The sermon from Jeremiah 7 which we examined above, with the listing of the sins of the people and the announcement of judgment, begins with a call to repentance: "Reform your ways and your actions, and I will let you live in this place" (v. 3; see also 17:9-13).

The book of Ecclesiastes talks a lot about the uncertainties of life. Unjust and foolish people succeed. The wise and righteous remain poor. It asks, is there any purpose in life? The crucial point of Ecclesiastes is in the last two verses of the book. Despite the uncertainties, the author urges his readers to "fear God and keep his commandments, for this is the whole duty of man" (Eccl. 12:13). How could he come up with such a conclusion after all the frustrating facts about righteous living that he had presented? The last verse solves this riddle: "For God will bring every deed into judgment, including every hidden thing, whether it is good or evil" (12:14). Judgment makes holy living sensible in today's world.

DESCRIBE JUDGMENT VIVIDLY

Most proclaimers of judgment in the Bible were very vivid in their descriptions of judgment. One example from Jeremiah would suffice to illustrate this:

> Your conduct and actions have brought this upon you. This is your punishment. How bitter it is! How it pierces to the heart! . . . I hear a cry as of a woman in labor, a groan as of one bearing her first child—the cry of the Daughter of Zion gasping for breath, stretching out her hand and saying, "Alas! I am fainting; my life is given over to murderers." (4:18, 31)

We are familiar with the vivid descriptions about hell and judgment that came from the lips of Jesus. He spoke about fire, about weeping and gnashing of teeth. He used the word "torment" to describe the suffering of hell (Luke 16:23, 28). However, the most vivid descriptions of judgment and hell are found in the book of Revelation, where a wealth of apocalyptic imagery is used to communicate the horror of judgment.

Is this the way we talk about hell today? If we talk about it at all, it is in a very restrained tone. Indeed, there needs to be restraint in making speculations about the nature of hell. But there is no restraint in the biblical descriptions of the horror of hell. We have a responsibility to warn people that it will be a horrible place. It is not enough to describe hell as separation from God, because our hearers may have consciously chosen to live separate from God. To them that would be a blessing. We may need to use more vivid language to convince the sinner that hell is not a place any sane person would want to enter.

USE CREATIVITY IN PRESENTATION

If we are to be vivid in proclaiming judgment, we need to find creative ways of doing it. Creativity is particularly important today because the media often presents what we know to be sinful in a seductively attractive form. We have to win a hearing for our message—no mean task in this media-saturated age. We have to convince our audience that what we preach is true. Often in the media, anti-Christian messages are communicated through absorbing dramas and films. Should we not use the same art forms to present our message?

Most of Jeremiah's contemporaries were not interested enough to listen to his preaching. So God asked Jeremiah to use acted parables in his battle for the attention of his audience. Once he got a linen belt and wore it around his waist. Then he hid it in a place where it would be exposed to decay. A few days later when he collected it, "it was ruined and completely useless." This was used as a symbol of the judgment that would come upon Judah because it followed other gods (Jer. 13:1-11).

Jeremiah's lifestyle was to become a parable to the people. He was asked to be single, something highly unusual for a normal adult man in Jeremiah's time (Jer .16:1-4). God asked him not to go to a house of mourning or a house of feasting (16:5-9). In the East, even today, the failure to attend weddings and funerals of loved ones is considered very serious. This powerful means of communication was to be used to impress upon the people that something serious was going to happen.

God once asked Jeremiah to take a clay jar, gather some leading citizens of Jerusalem, and go to the garbage dump outside the city, the Valley of Ben Hinnom (from which we get the word for hell, *gehenna*, 19:1, 2). He was to describe the approaching judgment to these people (vv. 3-9). Then he was to break the jar while those who went with him were watching, and say to them, "This is what the Lord Almighty says: I will smash this nation and this city just as this potter's jar is smashed and cannot be repaired" (vv. 10, 11).

There is a challenge here to artists, musicians and writers. If they produce high-quality paintings, songs, novels, plays and the like using the art forms that the people are familiar with, and if they seek to win a non-Christian audience for their work, they may be able to penetrate spheres where no preacher would be tolerated.

There is a particular need today for stories that use allegory to describe judgment. The traditional words for judgment would not be used. But by reading or viewing these stories the thinking of people would become positively oriented towards accepting Christian concepts. Some people call this pre-evangelism. C. S. Lewis used the medium of allegory in *The Great Divorce*[7] to present a description of his ideas of judgment (some of which, unfortunately, may not be quite in keeping with the teachings of the Bible).

Preaching is also an art. Preachers too may, like Jesus and the biblical writers, use allegories, parables, stories and the like to challenge people with the message of judgment.

Preachers must, however, not try to manipulate their audiences with emotionally charged stories and then invite them to make a public commitment to Christ. Some respond to such invitations without intelligently thinking about what they are doing because they are so emotionally moved by the story. Such manipulation of emotions has brought great disrepute to the gospel, especially to the message of judgment.

ALWAYS WORK FOR A GODWARD RESPONSE

Our aim in preaching on judgment is to help people to respond to God's call to repentance or to perseverance in discipleship. We see this call all the time in the preaching of Jeremiah. Even though he was called to proclaim an inevitable judgment that was soon to take place, he always challenged his audience to repent.[8]

MENTION JUDGMENT AS A POINT OF A LARGER MESSAGE

In Christian preaching, the key message that leads to repentance and discipleship is grace and not judgment. The message of judgment alerts the sinner to his *need* for salvation. The message of grace proclaims the *way* of salvation.

This may not be too evident in Jeremiah. Other than in chapters 31 and 32, which look forward to the restoration of the people, grace seems to be presented almost as an aside in this book. This is because Jeremiah spoke under special circumstances. He was speaking to a people who had been lulled into moral apathy by false prophets who preached grace without repentance. The people were relying on God's grace to save them. They needed to hear that the God of saving grace was also the God of judging holiness.

Jeremiah was called to fill a gap in the thinking of a people who had ignored God's holiness and judgment. There may be some today, too, who have such a call, given the strange silence about hell in the church. But generally we are called to major on grace.

A look at Jesus' teaching on hell suggests that hell was generally not the major focus in his discourses. He used it as a step along a path to his great goal of motivating people to repentance and discipleship. Often it provides the antithesis of or alternative to the main theme, which may be salvation or repentance or the Kingdom of God. John 3:16 says that those who believe in Christ "shall not perish but have eternal life." John 5:24 says that such a person "has eternal life and will not be condemned; he has crossed over from death to life." These texts would have been so much weaker if their judgment portions had been left out. These portions were introduced, almost as an aside, while describing the path to salvation.

There is an important lesson here. If we put off mentioning judgment and hell until we preach a full-length sermon on it, people will hardly ever hear about it, for such sermons are few and far between. Then the chances of this doctrine having any impact on them will be very slim. If, on the other hand, we mention it often—in passing—when speaking about other topics, then they will be exposed to it often enough to be influenced by it. Because it comes as part of the wider picture they will see how it integrates with the rest of life. Hell will then not be some specialized topic that is brought up occasionally, but something that has been integrated into our thinking about life. It will be part of our worldview.

In the evangelical movement today there are people who will sign a statement of faith that affirms the doctrine of hell but who have not assimilated their belief into their worldview. So it does not appear in their preaching and teaching. They will help mold the next generation of Christians into a group that does not know this doctrine. It will be easy for this generation to reject the doctrine completely. When one generation neglects the doctrine of hell, the next generation will reject it.

INCLUDE JUDGMENT IN CONVERSATIONS

Some of Jesus' teaching on hell came in his ordinary dialogue with people. We too need to introduce talk about hell into our conversations. As Jesus warned people, so should we. This is something that must appear in the conversation of parents with their children, for example.

When speaking to stubborn people, we may be called upon to make firm threats, as Jesus did in Matthew 23. This is where he tells the leaders, "Woe to you . . . you hypocrites!. . . . You snakes! You brood of vipers! How will you escape being condemned to hell?" (Matt. 23:29, 33). Now the sinless Christ, who knew what was in the heart of man, could say this with confidence. We cannot have such confidence. So we must be cautious about how we condemn people. But we can conclude from the statements of Matthew 23 that we must forthrightly challenge hypocrites about their hypocrisy and the judgment that it merits.

CHAPTER FIFTEEN

THE HERALD OF
JUDGMENT

What is a herald of judgment like? The "hellfire and damnation" preacher appears in the media as an eccentric and unpleasant person with whom no Christian likes to be compared. We will again use the life and ministry of Jeremiah to see what a biblical herald of judgment is like.

PROCLAIM JUDGMENT FAITHFULLY

In Jeremiah's time judgment was not a popular message and was a stark contrast to the attractive preaching of the false prophets. God said of the latter, "They dress the wound of my people as though it were not serious. 'Peace, peace,' they say, when there is no peace" (Jer. 8:11). Jeremiah would have liked to give such a message. When a false prophet once preached a soothing message of immediate restoration, Jeremiah responded, "Amen! May the Lord do so! May the Lord fulfill the words you have prophesied" (Jer. 28:6). But he went on to say that it will not be so. Once, after receiving a vision of the coming restoration, he expressed his delight over that message thus: "At this I awoke and looked around. My sleep had been pleasant to me" (Jer. 31:26).

However, Jeremiah was called to proclaim the message of judgment for most of his ministry. This message caused him to be alienated from others. He explained his life thus: "I never sat in the company of revelers, never made merry with them; I sat alone because your hand was on me and you had filled me with indignation" (Jer. 15:17). He then said, "Why is my pain unending and my wound grievous and incurable? Will you be to me like a deceptive brook, like a spring that fails?" (15:18). He did not like to be unpopular. Because of it he expressed the wish that he had never been born: "Alas, my mother, that you gave me birth, a man with whom the whole land strives and contends! I have neither lent nor borrowed, yet everyone curses me" (15:10).

If a contemporary minister were to speak like this, we would probably send him for specialized counseling or recommend that he change jobs. According to contemporary understandings of fulfillment in ministry, which comes more from the world than from the Scriptures, Jeremiah would undoubtedly be judged as unfulfilled and in the wrong type of work.

But through him came some of the most sublime heights of the Old Testament revelation. Paul expressed similar sentiments. Yet both Jeremiah and Paul have such a high place in the Bible *because they were faithful to their call.* They were not personally attracted to the difficult messages they were asked to give, but they faithfully gave them.

Once, after a particularly humiliating beating and overnight stay in stocks in a public place, Jeremiah complained bitterly to God, "O Lord, you deceived me, and I was deceived; you overpowered me and prevailed. I am ridiculed all day long; everyone mocks me. . . . So the word of the Lord has brought me insult and reproach all day long" (20:7, 8). But Jeremiah realized that he could not give up preaching this message: "But if I say, 'I will not mention him or speak any more in his name,' his word is in my heart like a burning fire, shut up in my bones. I am weary of holding it in; indeed, I cannot" (20:9). There was the constraint of divine anointing which caused Jeremiah to persevere despite the suffering.

If we preach judgment today, we too might encounter opposition. More than one pastor has told me that they had some members leave their churches after they preached a sermon on hell.

Ours, even more than Jeremiah's, is a "feel good" generation. The entertainment industry is flourishing. Society has turned so competitive and fast-paced that people live under great pressure. Entertainment provides an opportunity to release some of this pressure.

The theory that people must be entertained seems to have influenced church programming too. Sermons which make people feel good draw crowds. Books which entertain the readers sell well. So we concentrate on such. The more unpleasant teachings of Christianity can be kept for "the Wednesday night meeting," which less than 10 percent of the congregation usually attends. The Sunday service is dedicated to making people feel good. This in turn will make church attractive to people who want just enough religion to make them feel good about their religious life. The result is numerical "church growth." The message devoid of judgment seems to work in helping our churches "grow." And, strategists argue, if it works, it must be right!

In many circles the measure of the success of a minister is the numerical growth of his congregation. One who preaches judgment may not see such growth. So he may be considered a failure. "Failure" in one's career is one of the hardest experiences to endure. This is why preaching judgment is not easy today.

Yet a gospel devoid of judgment is not really effective, though it may produce numerical church growth. People have joined the church in response to a gospel that does not include hell. They might have rejected Christianity if they'd known that hell was part of the essential gospel. They came to Christ because it felt good to do so. The doctrine of hell does not feel good. It reminds people of the stress and pressure from which they want to be free.

So we will have large numbers of "half-baked Christians" in the church. They will not take up the cross to follow Christ into difficult places. They would rather compromise than suffer. These Christians are not the people who can turn the world upside-down. The church has grown, but that growth has been a fattening. It has lost its vitality and is helpless as an agent of lasting change in the world.

Besides, people who join churches by responding to an inadequate gospel will not find the freedom they seek. The greatest freedom one could experience is a realistic freedom—one based not simply on feeling good but on facts. The facts of the gospel include the stark reality of sin and its terrible consequences. People have to be told that. But that is done only as a prelude to presenting the glorious truth of God's grace, which is greater than their sin.

Those who know that they have received freedom from the terrible consequences of sin will be so grateful for this that they will be willing to deny themselves, take up the cross, and follow Christ wherever he leads them. The faithful proclamation of the "whole counsel of God" begets faithful followers of Christ.

I must quickly add that some churches that preach the whole counsel of God, including the unpleasant parts, have also seen large numerical growth. This is because of God's blessing. Numerical church growth is important to God because he loves the lost and wants to see them converted. When large numbers are converted, the glory to his name is great. The book of Acts gives the numbers of those who were converted at the start of the church in Jerusalem because numbers are significant. But we must never compromise the gospel in order to get large numbers.

When we are terrified by the hostility of our audience to our message, let us remember God's words to Jeremiah: "Get yourself ready! Stand up and say to them whatever I command you. Do not be terrified by them, or I will terrify you before them" (Jer. 1:17). Jeremiah is told that if he loses courage, God himself will shatter Jeremiah before his audience! If he is afraid of people, he will have to be afraid of falling into the hands of God, which is much more terrifying.

It may be that we ourselves will always be uncomfortable with the message of judgment. This is, firstly, because of the paradox of what we wish for people (their salvation) and what we tell them they will face if they do not repent (damnation). Secondly, given the importance of love in the Christian life, we would like to give a message that feels like a loving message. A message of judgment does not have that feel, even though warning people is a very loving thing to do.

Preachers have told me how emotionally difficult it was for them to preach about judgment. That is to be expected. We should not, however, measure success in ministry according to the extent to which we are comfortable with what we do. Charles Spurgeon has observed that some say, "I could not rest comfortably if I believed the orthodox doctrine about the ruin of men." Spurgeon's response to this is, "Most true. But what right have we to rest comfortably?"[1] We can have our comforts when we get to heaven. While we are on earth, let us concentrate on being faithful and let that determination counter the modern craze for shallow earthly fulfillment and comfort which has infiltrated our ideas of ministry.

REFLECT GOD'S HOLINESS

As representatives of God, Christians are called to reflect God's nature on earth. The Bible portrays God's nature as being holy love. The herald of judgment must also demonstrate this dual nature. We first look at the call to be holy.

Proclaiming Judgment Assuredly

One way God's holiness is manifested is in his unaccommodating opposition to sin. There is no wavering in God's mind about the dangerous consequences of sin. Therefore the message of judgment must be proclaimed assuredly. Jeremiah presented the message that his people would be punished without any compromise. When Jeremiah complained about the message of judgment, it was to himself or to God (Jer. 15:10, 15-18; 20:7-10, 14-18). He did not preach his doubts about what God revealed to him.

It is not unusual for the herald of God to have doubts about the message he is called to proclaim. Though Jeremiah had such doubts, he did not glory in them and proudly parade them in public, as some are prone to do today. Neither did Jeremiah remain complacent about the doubts. He grappled with them. Some who have doubts are too lazy to wrestle with them. So they learn to go on with life without troubling themselves with trying to find an answer. They either do not talk about the topic or they proclaim the doubts publicly.

Others are afraid of the doubts they have. They proclaim the message even though they have doubts about it. Their insecurity manifests itself in the powerlessness of the message they present. Some who have unresolved doubts try to compensate for it by assuming an authoritarian manner. Others, because of their doubts, proclaim the message in a very timid manner.

As a result of grappling with his doubts Jeremiah emerged with the deep and sensitive faith that has made his book one of the greatest classics of religious literature in human history. Grappling will give depth and richness to one's message. It gives a sensitivity to the questions people ask that makes the message relevant to the human situation and therefore more penetrative in its impact. It also gives an authority to the message that helps provide a base for stability to the bewildered people living in this age of uncertainty. Some great preachers like Billy Graham and G. Campbell Morgan went through agonizing periods of doubt at some stage of their lives. They came out stronger because of the battle they carried out. May I urge those struggling with the doctrine of hell to initiate a process of grappling with it.

Of course, we can be sure only of what God has revealed. There is much about judgment that he has not revealed. On those matters we must say that we do not know the answer. We should not be afraid of this. Some preachers today feel that because heralds of God must have an authoritative message, they must never betray the fact that they have some unanswered questions. Their commitment is to authority. But our commitment should be to truth. God has revealed truth in his Word. We proclaim that truth with authority.

What a contrast this is to the timidity we see in discourses on the topic of judgment today. Some who mention it say that they don't like to talk about it and that they wish it were not true, but because the Bible teaches it, they are obliged to say something about it. Charles Spurgeon says he heard of a minister who told his congregation, "If you do not love the Lord Jesus Christ, you will be sent to the place which it is not polite to mention." Spurgeon's comment on this was that "he ought not to have been allowed to preach again . . . for he could not use plain words."[2]

Sometimes Proclaiming Judgment Angrily

Our respect for people sometimes expresses itself in anger. This is not the selfish anger which results from ourselves being annoyed or inconvenienced. This is the anger that comes from seeing God dishonored by people who insult God and themselves by acting contrary to their true humanity. Its source is love for God and his honor and also love for the sinner.

Sometimes, even though we are angry because God has been dishonored, we may restrain ourselves and not express that anger publicly. In Athens Paul's "whole soul was revolted at the sight of a city given over to idolatry" (Acts 17:16, JB). But he did not express his revulsion publicly. Rather he "reasoned" with the people (17:17). These people were ignorant of the truth. They had to be informed of this truth and persuaded of its validity.

But when Paul encountered Elymas the sorcerer in Cyprus, he reacted very differently. This man "tried to turn the [Roman] proconsul from the faith." Luke tells us that

> Saul . . . filled with the Holy Spirit, looked straight at Elymas and said, "You are a child of the devil and an enemy of everything that is right! You are full of all kinds of deceit and trickery. Will you never stop perverting the right ways of the Lord? Now the hand of the Lord is against you. You are going to be blind, and for a time you will be unable to see the light of the sun." (Acts 13:8-11)

Elymas had perverted the truth, and for him there were angry words of judgment.

Paul's anger is described here as the result of being "filled with the Holy Spirit." This is similar to Christ's cleansing of the temple, which led his disciples to comment on Christ's zeal for God's house (John 2:17). The anger of Christ and Paul had left an impression of godliness.

Jeremiah, too, had times of righteous wrath. He says, "I am full of the wrath of the Lord, and I cannot hold it in." This anger was because "their ears are closed so they cannot hear. The word of the Lord is offensive to them; they find no pleasure in it" (6:10, 11).

The theme that runs through these texts is that we express anger over the hardheartedness of people who suppress the truth so that they can continue in their sinfulness. Over and over again Jeremiah mentions the people's unwillingness to listen to his message (6:10; 18:18; 19:15; 22:21).

We not only condemn the sins of the hardhearted—we also condemn the sinners themselves. Their biggest problem is not their actions but their heart attitude. They do not want to change even when they know the truth. This is why Jesus did not only condemn the actions of the Pharisees, he condemned them as persons. He once said, "You snakes! You brood of vipers! How will you escape being condemned to hell?" (Matt. 23:33).

Warning People About False Teachers

Another call coming from the holiness of God is to warn people about false teachers. Jeremiah did this about the false prophets. He says, "Do not listen to the prophets who say, 'Very soon now the articles from the Lord's house will be brought back from Babylon.' They are prophesying lies to you. Do not listen to them" (Jer. 27:16, 17; see also 5:30, 31; 6:13-15; 23:9-30). Similarly, Paul often warns believers to be careful of false teachers.[3]

Hebrews records the doctrine of "eternal judgment" as one of six basic tenets of Christian teaching (6:1, 2). If so, we must warn people about those who do not believe this doctrine. They must not be allowed to teach in the church. Like Paul (1 Cor. 15; Gal. 1—5; 1 Tim. 4), we must publicly refute their doctrines.

This attitude of opposition to false teaching is spurned by many Christians today, especially those who emphasize pluralism. Some of my fellow Methodists appeal to John Wesley's statement, "We think and let think," where Wesley advocated a type of pluralism. They forget that this statement comes as the second part of a larger sentence which reads, "But as to all *opinions which do not strike at the root of Christianity*, we think and let think" (italics mine). Wesley applies pluralism only to non-foundational matters. We cannot compromise on the fundamentals of the faith.

REFLECT GOD'S LOVE

As representatives of the God of holy love, our lives and ministries must also be characterized by love.

Concern for the Lost

God's love is expressed in the fact that he does not want "anyone to perish, but everyone to come to repentance" (2 Pet. 3:9; see also 1 Tim. 2:4). Jeremiah's love for his people was so intense that he was often emotionally broken over their fate. He says,

> Since my people are crushed, I am crushed; I mourn, and horror grips me. Is there no balm in Gilead? Is there no physician there? Why then is there no healing for the wound of my people? Oh, that my head were a spring of water and my eyes a fountain of tears! I would weep day and night for the slain of my people. (8:21–9:2; see also 9:10; 13:17; 14:17)

Jesus had "compassion on [the crowds], because they were harassed and helpless, like sheep without a shepherd" (Matt. 9:36). He wept when he pondered the fate of Jerusalem (Luke 19:41, 42). Tears were a common feature of the ministry of Paul (Acts 20:19, 31; Phil. 3:18). On the lostness of the Jews, he said, "I have great sorrow and unceasing anguish in my heart. For I could wish that I myself were cursed and cut off from Christ for the sake of . . . the people of Israel" (Rom. 9:2-4). So we, too, should have this brokenness over the predicament of people.

The British preacher R. W. Dale, who had departed somewhat from the orthodox doctrine of hell, once told Campbell Morgan, "I have never heard [D. L.] Moody refer to hell without tears in his voice." If this was true of Moody, it was indeed an admirable trait. But Dr. Dale went on to say that D. L. Moody was the only preacher he had ever heard who had the right to preach about hell. Many people today agree with this claim and say that because they were unable to speak about hell in the way Moody did, they will not speak about it at all.

I suspect that Moody's supposed "teary preaching" had much

to do with his personality. Some people express their emotions more readily than others. Therefore, it would be wrong to take this as a norm for legitimate preaching on hell. We have already shown that while sometimes the prospect of judgment elicited tears from biblical characters, at other times this proclamation was associated with anger. Sometimes it was associated with rational reasoning for the reality of retribution, without much outward expression of emotion.

Brokenness over lostness is not something we conjure up each time we preach on judgment. It is a constant state of mind which expresses itself not so much when we preach judgment as when we are reminded of people's lostness through some circumstance. Paul's outburst, mentioned above, was a prelude to a theological discussion on the salvation of the Jews (Rom. 9–11). The references to Christ's sorrow were sparked off by observations he made, once of the helpless crowd and the other time of the beautiful city of Jerusalem. Paul mentions that his anguish for the Jews was "unceasing." Yet elsewhere he talks of unceasing joy (Phil. 4:4). His sorrow over people's lostness was able to coexist with his joy in the Lord.

Even if we feel that we don't know the right way to talk about hell, the situation is so urgent that we can't wait till we straighten that out. An employee, detecting a fire in his office building, does not remain there without informing others because he feels he does not know the right way to say it. While that sounds ridiculous, we seem to use that same logic to excuse our silence about the much more serious fires of eternal judgment.

Love makes us warn people about hell. Love is the attitude we need for this work. Whether or not it manifests itself in literal tears is a secondary point.

Loved by God

The love we have for the lost is not something produced by our efforts. It is something given to us by God. "We love because he first loved us" (1 John 4:19). One of the greatest benefits of this love is our own identity and security as beloved children of God. John expressed his amazement over this when he exclaimed, "How great is the love the Father has lavished on us, that we should be called children of God" (1 John 3:1). When we think about our security as children of God, we would be overwhelmed with gratitude to God. Gratitude and pride cannot exist together. Gratitude focuses attention on someone else. Pride focuses on oneself. So one filled with love cannot be arrogant about his position as a child of God.

Such security in God is necessary for anyone who preaches judgment. The history of preaching is full of examples of insecure people who used the message of hell to boost their flagging sense of identity and significance. They condemned those who seemed to enjoy the life of sin. By arrogantly putting down sinners, they sought to put themselves up. These are the "hell-fire and damnation preachers" who have discredited the practice of preaching on hell. They lacked the humility and graciousness that comes from being filled with the love of God. Those who heard them saw their anger, but they did not see a love which would attract them to Christ.

Before God called Jeremiah to be a herald of judgment, he invested him with an identity as God's chosen vessel. He stunned Jeremiah with the pronouncement, "Before I formed you in the womb I knew you, before you were born I set you apart; I appointed you as a prophet to the nations" (Jer. 1:5). When Jeremiah protested, mentioning his inadequacy, God refuted that and asked him to be obedient (1:6, 7). Then he assured him, saying, "Do not be afraid . . . for I am with you and will rescue you" (1:8). Then the Lord reached out his hand and touched Jeremiah's mouth and said to him, "I have put my words in your mouth. See, today I appoint you over nations and kingdoms . . ." (1:9, 10).

Later, during a time of great discouragement, Jeremiah reminisced on the call and said, "When your words came, I ate them;

they were my joy and my heart's delight, for I bear your name, O Lord God Almighty" (15:16). His identity in God helped him weather the storms of loneliness and rejection that he faced because of his call. People like this, who are secure in God, can proclaim the judgment of God graciously.

A LIFESTYLE OF SERIOUSNESS

Holy love is a sober love. Biblical love has been sobered by the knowledge of the awful consequences of sin. The predicament of the human race brings on an urgency and seriousness that colors the way we live.

Today *hell* is a slang word in many societies. That is one evidence of how far we have moved from this seriousness. Psychologists say that when people don't know how to handle a problem, they sometimes compensate for their sense of insecurity by making a joke of the issue. I wonder whether this is how hell took on such a lighthearted flavor in general conversation. Certainly the entertainment orientation of people and the flippancy with which some people approach the serious things in life may indicate that humanity is trying to suppress a gnawing sense that something is seriously wrong.

Experienced counselors also tell us that when people try to escape the reality of their situation, it is important to gently bring them to the point of facing up to it honestly. This is our aim as witnesses. We are loving, and we are serious, in that we are open for lengthy discussions on the issues that matter most in life. This seriousness commends reality to others.

Our priorities in life also serve as a challenge to the world, which is depending for fulfillment on things that do not satisfy. The rich long for their fun-filled use of leisure times. Our concern for such people, coupled with our lifestyle that is blatantly eternity-oriented, could be a challenge to them. When they get disillusioned by the shallow satisfaction earthly pleasures bring, they may look for answers to the eternal issues of life.

The poor in this new society have experienced what has been called "the revolution of rising expectations." They have come to believe that all people could prosper if only they used the right means to gain wealth. So now they too have fallen victim to the trap of materialism. We show genuine concern to such people also. Our lifestyle demonstrates the fact that when one seeks first the Kingdom of God, all that is necessary for a contented life will be added as well. We share with them the message of Christ. This combination of concern, example and verbal witness could be what challenges them to realize that the greatest achievements are those that are of eternal significance.

What we are describing here is a prophetic lifestyle that is able to challenge the rich and the poor and show them that what they need is the unshakable security of a home in heaven. We work hard in society but are not slaves to the rat race that causes people to break principles in order to get earthly success. We are concerned for our personal welfare, but we love our neighbors as ourselves. We enjoy a good joke, but we are also able to sit down and have a long, serious chat. We are not against material things, but we reject opulence, even if it were available to us, and opt for a lifestyle of simplicity which commends a beauty that finds its deepest joys in eternal values. This prophetic lifestyle points people to the eternal dimension.

Our society is dedicated to the pursuit of earthly pleasure, and even many of our church programs are designed to pander to this pursuit. In such an environment a serious individual may feel out of place. A prophetic lifestyle usually elicits the disdain of worldly people. This was the experience of Jeremiah. It was also the experience of the most famous expounder of judgment in the modern era, Jonathan Edwards. He was dismissed from the church he pastored for over two decades, partly because of the unpleasant aspects of the gospel that he insisted should be practiced by the church. Yet today he is regarded by many as the greatest philosopher that America produced. Let us not be discouraged by rejection.

A LIFESTYLE OF MORAL PURITY

A key aspect of the holiness of the herald of judgment is moral purity. I can think of three ways in which holiness of life affects the proclamation of judgment. Firstly, the preaching of judgment is a direct attack on sin. If so, the herald of that message must know victory over sin. The life is what adds credibility to the message. It demonstrates to the world that the repentance proclaimed can indeed take place.

Secondly, a holy life gives the herald a quiet confidence in God which gives great power to proclamation. The relationship between the herald and God is open and warm. There is no hindrance to being filled with the Holy Spirit and his power. The combination of conviction over the message and the confidence that comes from contact with God can help convince the sinner to listen to the message. By observing the herald, he could infer that this person has found true fulfillment in life. Then the Holy Spirit can freely do his work of conviction.

Thirdly, a holy life is the best insurance against the vulnerability to attack and criticism that a herald of judgment will invariably encounter. People don't generally like to hear that they are sinners headed for judgment. So they will try to oppose the message in some way. A common way to do so is to point to sin in the herald's life. None of us is immune to such accusations. But if our testimony is clear, those voices will not have permanent power.

Jeremiah could claim that he was beyond reproach, but despite that he was often accused by his opponents. He mourned, "Alas, my mother, that you gave me birth, a man with whom the whole land strives and contends! I have neither lent nor borrowed, yet everyone curses me. . . . I never sat in the company of revelers, never made merry with them; I sat alone because your hand was on me" (Jer. 15:10, 17). But because Jeremiah lived what he preached, his ministry has stood the test of time.

We live in an age when orthodoxy and holiness of life do not always go together. In recent years some of the champions of orthodoxy have been exposed as being immoral in their personal lives. Some of these fallen preachers became identified as champions because they denounced sin and proclaimed judgment. They won many sincere followers from among Christians who are enraged by the deteriorating morals in contemporary society. So the ministries of these "unholy heralds" flourished for a time, and their fall brought great dishonor to the name of Christ.

A PART OF THE GOOD NEWS

We bring this book to a close by stating again that judgment is not our main message. It is a step along the path to proclaiming the good news. If our hearers don't realize that there is a judgment to come, they may not see the need to be saved and thus not realize the goodness of the good news. They will say that they would prefer to rule their lives and seek to find salvation by their own ways. The message of judgment arrests them so that they would sense their need for a Savior. So it is part of the good news!

NOTES

INTRODUCTION

1. *A Universal Homecoming? An Examination of the Case for Universalism* (Madras: ELS, 1983).

CHAPTER ONE: *The Decline of Hell*

1. This is the title of a book by D. P. Walker (Chicago: The University of Chicago Press, 1964).
2. *Evangelical Theology 2* (San Francisco: Harper & Row, 1978), p. 211.
3. Reported in *Newsweek* (April 3, 1989), p. 44.
4. *Heaven and Hell* (Nashville: Thomas Nelson, 1986), p. 174.

CHAPTER TWO: *What Will Hell Be Like?*

1. Matthew 5:22, 29, 30; 10:28; 18:9; 23:15, 33; Mark 9:43, 45, 47; Luke 12:5.
2. Second edition (Chicago: The University of Chicago Press, 1979), p. 134.

CHAPTER THREE: *What About Annihilationism?*

1. See, for example, *New Bible Dictionary*, second edition, revised edition, ed. N. Hillyer (Leicester, England: IVP, 1982), p. 473; Stephen Travis, *I Believe in the Second Coming of Jesus* (Grand Rapids, Mich.: Wm. B. Eerdmans [British edition: London: Hodder and Stoughton], 1982), pp. 198, 199.
2. Clark Pinnock, "Fire, Then Nothing," *Christianity Today* (March 20, 1987), p. 41.
3. See John Stott, *Essentials* (London: Hodder & Stoughton, 1988), p. 316.
4. *Ibid.*, p. 318.
5. *The Wages of Sin* (London: Tyndale Press, 1955), p. 22.

CHAPTER FOUR: *How Long Will Hell Last?*

1. *A Spiritual Autobiography* (Grand Rapids, Mich.: Wm. B. Eerdmans, 1975), p. 60.
2. *The Future Life*, trans. Helen I. Needham (Chicago: Moody Press, 1962), p. 293.
3. *Christian Understanding of God* (New York: Harper & Bros., 1951), p. 244.
4. *New Testament Theology*, trans. John Marsh (London: SCM Press, 1955), pp. 222-231.
5. *Outlines of Theology* (Grand Rapids, Mich.: Wm. B. Eerdmans, reprint of 1879 edition), p. 581.
6. *Autobiography*, p. 60.
7. *Tyndale New Testament Commentaries: Luke*, revised edition (Leicester, England: IVP and Grand Rapids, Mich.: Wm. B. Eerdmans, 1988), p. 277.
8. *Systematic Theology* (Valley Forge, Penn.: Judson Press, reprint of 1907 edition), p. 1043.
9. For example, the commentaries by Edwin A. Blum, J. N. D. Kelley, J. Ramsey Michaels, and Edward G. Selwyn and the special studies by William J. Dalton, *Christ's Proclamation to the Spirits* (Rome: Pontifical Biblical Institute, 1965) and R. T. France, "Exegesis in Practice: Two Samples," *New Testament Interpretation*, ed. I. Howard Marshall (Grand Rapids, Mich.: Wm. B. Eerdmans, 1977), pp. 264-276, originally published by Exeter, England: The Paternoster Press Ltd., 1977.
10. *Tyndale New Testament Commentaries: The First Epistle of Peter* (Leicester, England: IVP and Grand Rapids,Mich.: Wm. B. Eerdmans, 1988), pp. 157-162, 203-239.
11. *First Epistle of Peter*, p. 172.
12. I have discussed the above two texts from 1 Peter in greater detail in my book *Jesus and the World Religions* (Eastbourne, England: MARC and Bromley, England: STL Books, 1988; American edition: *The Christian's Attitude Toward World Religions* [Wheaton, Ill.: Tyndale House, 1987]), pp. 140-144.
13. *A Critical and Exegetical Commentary on the First Epistle of St Paul to the Corinthians*, second edition (Edinburgh: T. & T. Clark, 1914), p. 359.

CHAPTER FIVE: *The Universal Savior of the World*

1. For a detailed study of the biblical arguments used by universalists see my *A Universal Homecoming? An Examination of the Case for Universalism* (Madras: ELS, 1983).
2. "Universalism and the Worldwide Community," *Churchman*, Vol. 89 (July-September 1975), p. 201.

3. *Word Pictures in the New Testament*, Vol. V (New York and London: Harper & Bros., 1932), p. 229.

4. *Christ and Adam: Man and Humanity in Romans 5*, trans. T. A. Smail (New York: Macmillan, 1968, reprint of 1957 edition), p. 31.

5. *Ibid.*, p. 23 (my italics).

6. *Church Dogmatics* II, 2: *The Doctrine of God*, trans. G. W. Bromiley and others (Edinburgh: T. & T. Clark, 1957), p. 346.

7. *Ibid.*, p. 352.

8. This point is made in Henri Blocher, "The Lost State of Man," *Evangelism Alert*, ed. Gilbert W. Kirby (London: World Wide Publications, 1972), pp. 55, 56; and Bernard Ramm, "Will All Men Be Finally Saved?," *Eternity* (August 1964), p. 23.

9. *The Christian Faith*, trans. (from German edition of 1930) and ed. H. R. Mackintosh and J. S. Stewart (New York: Harper & Row, reprinted 1963), p. 558.

10. *Ibid.*, p. 560.

11. *Shaking the Sleeping Beauty* (Leicester, England: IVP, 1980), p. 133.

CHAPTER SIX: *Will Christ's Final Victory Be Incomplete?*

1. "The Idea of Immortality in Relation to Religion and Ethics" (Drew Lecture, 1931, Independent Press, 1932). Cited in Michael Griffiths, *Shaking the Sleeping Beauty* (Leicester, England: IVP, 1980), p. 116.

2. See John Jefferson Davis, *Christ's Victorious Kingdom* (Grand Rapids, Mich.: Baker Book House, 1986). I am indebted to this book for many points in this section.

3. (Nairobi: Oxford University Press, 1982), p. 19.

4. *The Christian Outlook* (New York: Harper & Row, 1948), p. 194.

5. For a detailed examination of these texts see my book, *A Universal Homecoming? An Examination of the Case for Universalism* (Madras: ELS, 1983), pp. 120-132.

6. *Evil and the Christian Faith* (New York and London: Harper & Bros., 1947), p. 119.

7. *New Testament Theology*, trans. John Marsh (London: SCM Press, 1955), pp. 222-231.

8. *An Expanded Paraphrase of the Epistles of Paul* (Palm Springs, Calif.: Ronald Haynes Publishers, 1981), p. 231.

9. *The Epistles to the Colossians, to Philemon and to the Ephesians* (Grand Rapids: Wm. B. Eerdmans, 1984), p. 75.

10. *Colossians*, p. 76.

11. See M. M. Thomas, *The Acknowledged Christ of the Indian Renaissance* (London: SCM Press, 1969), p. 61.

12. *Keshub Chandra Sen's Lectures in India* (London: The Brahmo Samaj, Cassell, 1909), p. 14; cited in Robin Boyd, *An Introduction to Indian Christian Theology* (Madras: ELS, 1975), p. 28.
13. For a simplified description of de Chardin's thinking, see Doran McCarty, *Teilhard de Chardin* (Waco, Tex.: Word Books, 1976).

CHAPTER SEVEN: *What About Reincarnation?*

1. George Gallup, Jr., *Adventures in Immortality* (New York: McGraw-Hill, 1982), p. 192.
2. *The European Value System Study Group, 1986* (Philadelphia: Westminster Press, 1974), p. 51.
3. *Ibid.*
4. *Reincarnation for the Christian*, pp. 88-91.
5. *Ibid.*, p. 96.
6. *The Gospel of John* (Grand Rapids, Mich.: Wm. B. Eerdmans, 1983), pp. 208, 209, 221. First published in England by Pickering & Inglis, 1983.
7. *Reincarnation: A Christian Appraisal* (Downers Grove, Ill.: IVP, 1982), p. 69.
8. *Ibid.*, p. 62.
9. *Ibid.*, p. 64.
10. *Ibid.*, p. 71.
11. In a letter to the editor, *Christian Parapsychologist* (June 1980).
12. *Reincarnation as a Christian Hope* (Totowa, N.J.: Barnes and Noble Imports, 1982), p. 72.
13. Norman Geisler and Yutuka Amano, *The Reincarnation Sensation* (Wheaton, Ill.: Tyndale House, 1986), p. 111.
14. *Evil and the God of Love* (Glasgow: Collins, Fount Paperbacks, 1979 reprint of 1966 edition), p. 383.
15. See Stephen Travis, *Christian Hope and the Future* (Downers Grove, Ill.: IVP, 1980; British edition: Leicester, England: IVP, 1980), p. 131.
16. "Reincarnation: A Second Time Around," *Eternity* (October 1988), p. 68.

CHAPTER EIGHT: *God's Will to Save All*

1. Nels Ferre, *Evil and the Christian Faith* (New York and London: Harper & Bros, 1947), p. 118.
2. See also John Hick, *Evil and the God of Love* (Glasgow: Collins, Fount Paperbacks, 1979 reprint of 1966 edition), pp. 379-381.
3. *Studies in Dogmatics: The Return of Christ*, trans. J. Van Oosterom, ed. M. J. Van Elderen (Grand Rapids, Mich.: Wm. B. Eerdmans, 1972), p. 406.
4. *Evil and . . .* , p. 378.
5. *Ibid.*, p. 311.

6. "The First Principles," in *The Anti-Nicene Fathers* (Grand Rapids, Mich.: Wm. B. Eerdmans, 1976), p. 226.

7. "Can God Save Anyone He Will?," *Scottish Journal of Theology*, Vol. 38 (1985), p. 162.

CHAPTER NINE: *Is God Being Just and Fair?*

1. *The Christian Understanding of God* (New York: Harper & Bros., 1951), p. 228.

2. *Therefore Stand*, reprint (New Canaan, Conn.: Keats Publishing, 1981), p. 448.

3. *The Atonement* (Leicester, England and Downers Grove, Ill.: IVP, 1983), p. 177.

4. Leon Morris, *The Apostolic Preaching of the Cross* (Grand Rapids, Mich.: Wm. B. Eerdmans, 1955), p. 225.

5. *Systematic Theology* (Valley Forge, Penn.: Judson Press, reprint of 1907 edition), p. 293.

6. Cited in *Newsweek* (April 3, 1989), p. 43.

7. (New York: Hawthorn Books, 1973).

8. Constance E. Padwick, *Henry Martyn* (New York: George H. Doran Co., c. 1922), p. 167.

9. *The Book of Revelation* (Grand Rapids, Mich.: Wm. B. Eerdmans, 1977), p. 295.

10. In his forthcoming book on the unity of the Bible to which I am indebted for many concepts in this section.

11. *Christian Understanding*, p. 228.

12. See John Gerstner, *Jonathan Edwards on Heaven and Hell* (Grand Rapids, Mich.: Baker Book House, 1980), pp. 79-87.

13. On this, see my *Jesus and the World Religions* (Bromley, England: STL and Eastbourne, England: MARC, 1988; American edition: *The Christian's Attitude Toward World Religions* (Wheaton, Ill.: Tyndale House, 1987]), chapters 9, 10.

CHAPTER TEN: *Wrath versus God's Love*

1. *The Epistle of Paul to the Romans* (London: Hodder & Stoughton, 1932), p. 23.

2. *The Wrath of the Lamb* (London: SPCK, 1959), p. 69.

3. *Wrath*, p. 110.

4. *Romans*, p. 23.

5. *Ibid.*, p 176-187.

6. For a detailed description of this, see "*Orgē*," in Gustav Stahlin, *Theological Dictionary of the New Testament*, Vol. V, ed. Gerhard Friedrich, trans. and

ed. Geoffrey W. Bromiley (Grand Rapids, Mich.: Wm. B. Eerdmans, 1968), pp. 427-429.

7. *Ibid.*, p. 427.

8. *Sin, Studies in Dogmatics*, trans. Philip C. Holtrop (Grand Rapids, Mich.: Wm. B. Eerdmans, 1971), p. 355.

9. (Grand Rapids: Wm. B. Eerdmans. and London: The Tyndale Press, 1955), pp 125-185. See also his *The Atonement: Its Meaning and Significance* (Leicester, England and Downers Grove, Ill.: IVP, 1983), pp. 151-176.

10. *Atonement*, p. 173.

11. *Apostolic Preaching*, pp. 181, 182.

12. *Aspects of Christian Social Ethics* (Grand Rapids, Mich.: Wm. B. Eerdmans, 1964), p. 168.

13. *Evil and the Christian Faith* (New York and London: Harper & Bros, 1947), pp. 118, 119.

14. *The Biblical Doctrine of the Wrath of God* (London: The Tyndale Press, 1951), pp. 36, 37.

CHAPTER ELEVEN: *How Universalists Handle the Bible*

1. *The Bible Doctrine of the Hereafter* (London: The Epworth Press, 1958), p. 258.

2. "Towards a Biblical View of Universalism," *Themelios*, Vol. 4 (1979), p. 55.

3. *Death and Eternal Life* (London: Collins, 1976), pp. 243-247.

4. "Universalism: a Historical Survey," *Themelios*, Vol. 4 (1979), p. 52.

5. *Death*, p. 249.

6. See *ibid.*, pp. 279-295.

7. "Universalism, Pro and Con," *Christianity Today* (March 1, 1963), p. 540. See also John A. T. Robinson, *In the End God* (New York: Harper & Row, 1968), p. 128.

8. *In the End*, p. 44 (numbers in brackets refer to page numbers in this book).

9. *Ibid.*, p. 46.

10. *Ibid.*, p. 128.

11. Ryder Smith, *Bible Doctrine*, pp. 256, 257.

12. Theodicy is the vindication of the justice of God in permitting evil to exist.

13. *God Has Many Names*, pp. 4, 5 (italics mine). Cited in Nigel M. de S. Cameron, "Universalism and the Logic of Revelation," *Evangelical Review of Theology*, Vol. 11, No. 4 (October 1987), p. 327.

14. *The Christian Understanding of God* (New York: Harper & Bros., 1951), p. 246.

15. *Evil and the Christian Faith* (New York & London: Harper & Bros., 1947), p. 118, 119.

16. *Christian Understanding*, p. 244.

17. *Evil and the God of Love* (London & Glasgow: Collins, Fount Paperbacks, 1979, reprint of 1979 edition), p. 382.
18. *The Attributes of God* (Grand Rapids: Baker Book House, reprinted 1975), p. 82 (his italics).
19. *The Humanity of God* (Richmond, Va.: John Knox Press, 1960), p. 61.
20. *Church Dogmatics*, II, 2, *The Doctrine of God*, trans. G. W. Bromiley and others (Edinburgh: T. & T. Clark, 1957), p. 422.
21. "Karl Barth," in *Creative Minds in Contemporary Theology*, ed. Philip E. Hughes (Grand Rapids, Mich.: Wm. B. Eerdmans, 1969), pp. 54, 55.

CHAPTER TWELVE: *Why Should We Talk About Judgment?*

1. Cited in Martin E. Marty, "Hell Disappeared. No One Noticed. A Civic Argument," *Harvard Theological Review*, Vol. 78 (3—4) (1985), p. 386.
2. Peter Toon, *Heaven and Hell* (Nashville: Thomas Nelson Publishers, 1986), pp. 29-46.
3. *And the Life Everlasting* (London, 1934), p. 294. Cited in N. T. Wright, "Universalism and the Worldwide Community," *The Churchman*, Vol. 89 (3) (1975), p. 203.
4. *The Judgment of the Dead* (London, 1967), pp. 193-196; cited in Wright, "Universalism," p. 203.
5. Marty, "Hell Disappeared," p. 386.

CHAPTER THIRTEEN: *Lostness as a Motivation to Evangelism*

1. "Universalism and the Worldwide Community," *The Churchman*, Vol. 89 (3) (1975), p. 204.
2. Cited in *The Letters of Samuel Rutherford*, ed. Frank E. Gaebelein (Chicago: Moody Press, reprinted 1980), p. 22.
3. Cited in Stanley N. Gundry, *Love Them in: The Life and Theology of D. L. Moody* (Grand Rapids, Mich.: Baker Book House, 1976), p 97, 98.
4. "A Look at Hell," *Preaching Today*, tape no. 28 (Carol Stream: Christianity Today).
5. See R. Pierce Beaver, "Missionary Motivation Through Three Centuries," in *Reinterpretation in American Church History*, ed. J. C. Brauer (Chicago: The University of Chicago Press, 1968), pp. 133-139.

CHAPTER FOURTEEN: *Proclaiming the Message of Judgment*

1. See Acts 17:4, 5, 17; 18:4; 19:8, 26; 24:24, 25; 26:25-28; 28:23.
2. Cited in *Spurgeon at His Best*, Tom Carter, compiler (Grand Rapids, Mich.: Baker Book House, 1988), p. 98.
3. Francis Schaeffer, in his book *The God Who Is There*, has a stimulating dis-

cussion on the type of reasoning I have been advocating, which he calls "taking the roof off" (Downers Grove, Ill.: IVP [British edition: London: Hodder and Stoughton Ltd.], 1968), pp. 128-130.

4. See Earle E. Cairns, *An Endless Line of Splendor* (Wheaton, Ill.: Tyndale House, 1986), pp. 320, 321.

5. Jeremiah 5:30, 31; 6:13-15; 14:14, 15; 23:9-40.

6. F. F. Bruce, *The Book of Acts* (Grand Rapids, Mich.: Wm. B. Eerdmans, 1988), pp, 340, 341.

7. (Glasgow: Collins, Fount Paperbacks, reprint of 1946 edition).

8. See Jeremiah 3:12-15, 22; 4:1-4; 7:2-7; 9:23, 24; 13:15-17; 17:7, 8; etc.

CHAPTER FIFTEEN: *The Herald of Judgment*

1. Cited in *Spurgeon at His Best*, Tom Carter, compiler (Grand Rapids, Mich.: Baker Book House, 1988), p. 99.

2. Cited in *ibid.*, p. 99.

3. See 2 Corinthians 11:1-13; Galatians 1:6-9; 1 Timothy 1:19, 20; 4:1-4, 7; 2 Timothy 4:3, 4, 15; Titus 1:9; 3:9-11.